STUDIES IN IMPERIALISM

general editor John M. MacKenzie

Established in the belief that imperialism as a cultural phenomenon had as significant an effect on the dominant as on the subordinate societies, Studies in Imperialism seeks to develop the new socio-cultural approach which has emerged through cross-disciplinary work on popular culture, media studies, art history, the study of education and religion, sports history, and children's literature. The cultural emphasis embraces studies of migration and race, while the older political, and constitutional, economic and military concerns will never be far away. It will incorporate comparative work on European and American empire-building, with the chronological focus primarily, though not exclusively, on the nineteenth and twentieth centuries, when these cultural exchanges were most powerfully at work.

RECRUITING for KITCHENER'S ARMY

THE STANDARD SERIES
MANUFACTURED IN DUNDEE, SCOTLAND.
BRITISH MANUFACTURE

REGISTRATION APPLIED FOR

At duty's call

A STUDY IN OBSOLETE
PATRIOTISM

W. J. Reader

MANCHESTER
UNIVERSITY PRESS

Manchester and New York

Distributed exclusively in the USA and Canada
by ST. MARTIN'S PRESS, New York

Copyright © W.J. Reader 1988

Published by MANCHESTER UNIVERSITY PRESS
Oxford Road, Manchester M13 9PL

Distributed exclusively in the USA and Canada by
ST. MARTIN'S PRESS, Room 400, 175 Fifth Avenue,
New York, NY 10010, USA

British Library cataloguing in publication data
Reader, W.J.
At Duty's call: a study in obsolete patriotism.—(Studies in imperialism).
1. Great Britain, Army —History —1914-1918
2. Military service, Voluntary —Social aspects—Great Britain—History—20th century
3. World War, 1914-1918—Social aspects—Great Britain
I. Title II. Series
306' .27'0941   D546

Library of Congress cataloging in publication data
Reader, W.J. (William Joseph), 1920-
At Duty's call: a study in obsolete patriotism/W.J. Reader
        p. cm—(Studies in imperialism)
    Bibliography: p. 135.
    Includes index.
ISBN 0-7190-2395-5 : $30.00 (est.)
1. Great Britain. Army—History—World War, 1914-1918. 2. Great Britain. Army—
Recruitment, enlistment, etc. 3. Patriotism—Great Britain—History—20th century. I. Title. II.
Series: Studies in imperialism (Manchester (Greater Manchester))
D546.R43 1988
940.0'12'41—dc19

ISBN 0 7190 2395 5 *hardback*

Printed in Great Britain
by Bell & Bain Limited, Glasgow

CONTENTS

LIST OF ILLUSTRATIONS

GENERAL EDITOR'S FOREWORD

Imperialism was more than a set of economic, political, and military phenomena. It was a habit of mind, a dominant idea in the era of European world supremacy which had widespread intellectual, cultural, and technical expressions. The 'Studies in Imperialism' series is designed to explore, primarily but not exclusively, these relatively neglected areas. Volumes are planned on the scientific aspects of imperialism, on education, disease, the theatre, literature, art, design, and many more. But in redressing the balance in favour of these multi-disciplinary and cross-cultural studies, it is not intended that the economic, political, and military dimensions should be ignored. The series will also contain books in these fields and will seek to examine colonial and imperial developments in a variety of periods and in diverse geographical contexts. It is hoped that individually and collectively these works will illumine one of the most potent characteristics of modern world history.

In this book W.J. Reader attempts to understand what he describes as 'one of the most extraordinary mass movements in history', the voluntary enlistment of two and a half million men in the British army in the first sixteen months of the Great War. He seeks to explore the cultural dimensions of the age which helped to form those volunteers' patriotism and their willingness to sacrifice themselves to defend a faith which allied a conviction about national superiority to a divine right to imperial rule. This ideology, national and international at the same time, had suffused popular entertainment, education, juvenile literature, the arts, and the press during the preceding decades. An entire generation had been brought up to a particular set of attitudes about war, a favourable view of the armed forces in British imperial life, a veneration for the monarchy, and a belief in the importance of the British Empire to the spread of civilisation across the globe. To this was added the paranoid Germanophobia of the pre-war years. The volunteers were, perhaps, influenced by a powerful set of interlocking ideas which our more sceptical and pluralistic age finds difficult to comprehend.

John M. MacKenzie

FOREWORD

This book is the result of reflection on one of the most extraordinary mass movements in history: the surge of volunteers - more than 2 ½ million - into the British army during the first sixteen months of the Great War. It will not, I think, be denied that this is one of the great tragic themes of recent British experience, but such a thorough demolition job has by now been done on traditional patriotism that it is difficult to comprehend what made it a force so powerful that it could propel so many men into one of the bloodiest wars ever fought without anything in the way of legal compulsion. I have tried to form a view of how various influences in the life of the nation combined, over a period of fifty years or so, into an exceedingly explosive mixture which was detonated on 4th August 1914.

I am grateful to John MacKenzie for including this book in his series. For first-hand accounts of what it felt like to be a young man when the Great War broke out I am indebted to Messrs M. Chapman, W. V. C. Maffett, S. Margetts, G. L. Smith, H. D. Till and T. R. Till - not all of whom, unfortunately, have lived to see the book in print - and to the staff of the Imperial War Museum for access to personal memoirs, recruiting posters and much other such material.

Brian Bond, Raymond and Mary Helen Callahan, Sheila Friend-Smith, Michael and Rachel Lawrence, Kathy Meek, Sylvia Southcombe and Charles Wilson have all done me the kindness to read and comment on the typescript and I should also like to thank J. R. de S. Honey for his comments on Chapter Five.

Finally, I owe a great deal to my wife's perceptive comments and to her assiduity in propelling me into numerous second-hand and antiquarian bookshops: indispensable research centres which, without her prompting, I should have neglected.

Cambridge   W. J. Reader
April 1987

CHAPTER ONE

'Their name liveth for evermore'

You need not usually go far, in British towns and villages, to find what local people call 'The War Memorial'. Perhaps the bus stops by it. Perhaps it is the centrepiece of a public park. Perhaps it stands in the main square, isolated by traffic. It is part of the civic furniture, like the statue of the Victorian mayor who donated the public baths or the statue of Queen Victoria put up to mark her Diamond Jubilee in 1897. In a village a 'memorial hall' may stand alongside it. These are memorials to one of the most remarkable mass movements of modern times, perhaps of any time: the enlistment of $2\frac{1}{2}$ million men of the United Kingdom and many more from the Empire, without any form of legal compulsion, from August 1914 to the end of 1915. There never was a volunteer army like it before. It seems safe to say there never will be again.

What brought that army into being?

That is the question which this book sets out to investigate, though not to answer, for no definitive answer is possible. No one can search the minds of $2\frac{1}{2}$ million men, most now dead and many in their lifetime inarticulate. What was it in the air of England, in the generation or so before August 1914, which brought about that collective exaltation which swept so many men willingly to war?

It must have been some unique concentration of forces, for most men at most times do not willingly become soldiers. Even in so free a society as the United States compulsion has been brought to bear and more or less willingly accepted when large armies have been required. Yet for a short time in Great Britain and her Empire compulsion was neither acceptable nor necessary. Men in millions came forward to enlist, not only the most numerous but probably the most enthusiastic volunteers the world has ever seen and, as their fighting record shows, brave and enduring also.

If nations, like individuals, sometimes go through periods of intense emotional strain - Americans during the Civil War, perhaps, and again during the Depression of the 1930's, or Germans during the inflation of 1923-24 - then the period of the Great War was certainly such a period for the British. Why, otherwise, would war memorials have been built in such numbers and why, otherwise, would they still be freshly garlanded, every November, with scarlet 'Flanders poppies'? To call it the 'Great War' is unfashionable to-day, but in the context of recent British history, and perhaps of European history also, no other form of words will do. Memorials to the Second World War are rare, except as more or less insignificant appendices to Great War memorials. Can we throw any light on the intensity of the British experience between 1914 and 1918 by focussing on one extraordinary phenomenon: the urge to 'join up'?

The dead of earlier wars, except here and there those of the South African War - the Boer War - of 1899-1902, were not commonly honoured with municipal memorials. If their names appear anywhere, it is likely to be on regimental memorials or on the walls of parish churches or cathedrals, as in the case of the twelve officers, two surgeons, nineteen sergeants, seventeen corporals, two drummers and 316 rank-and-file of the 80th Foot who lost their lives in Burma between March 1852 and November 1853 and are commemorated on a monument in Lichfield Cathedral. Apart from the officers, the only ones whose names are given are a colour-sergeant and nine privates killed in action. The anonymous remainder were 'carried off by cholera dysentery and other diseases of the country'. Disease killed far more soldiers, in all wars before the Great War, than the weapons of the enemy, and the names of 'other ranks' who died were rarely recorded.

Collective memorials earlier than the nineteenth century are exceedingly rare, though there is one at Clifton, Bristol, inscribed with stately eighteenth-century elegiac prose:

SACRED

To the Memory of those departed Warriors
Of the seventy-ninth Regiment
By whose Valour Discipline and Perseverance
The French Land Forces in Asia were first withstood and repulsed

...

Their generous Treatment
of a vanquish'd Enemy
Exhibits an illustrious Example
of true Fortitude and Moderation
worthy of being transmitted
To latest of Posterity
That future Generations may know
HUMANITY is the Characteristic
of BRITISH CONQUERORS.

The monument recalls campaigns of the Seven Years' War (1756-1763), including the capture of Manila. It was put up in his own garden by Lieutenant-General Sir William Draper (1721-1787), who raised the regiment. His later military career was clouded. He did not intend his early glories to be forgotten.

Memorials to individuals, as distinct from regimental memorials, go back much further, certainly to Queen Elizabeth I's wars in the Low Countries and to the English Civil War. 'HERE', says a wooden memorial at Horncastle, Lincolnshire, 'lieth ye worthy and memorable Kt Sr Ingram Hopton who paid his debt to nature & duty to his KING and COUNTRY - in the attempt of seising ye Arch-Rebel in the bloody Skirmish near Winceby, October ye 6 AD 1643' ('Ye Arch-Rebel' - Oliver Cromwell - was chivalrous enough to return Sir Ingram's body to his family for burial).

An eighteenth-century Rear-Admiral - Sir John Jennings (1664-1743) - is commemorated at Barkway in Cambridgeshire for 'The Share he had in taking the French Men of War and the Spanish Galleons at Vigo'. Of General Peregrine Lascelles it is recorded at Whitby that in 1745 'after a fruitless exertion of his spirit and ability at the disgracefull rout of Prestonpans he remained forsaken on the feild.' At Shapwick, in Somerset, two memorial tablets recall the taking of the *Kent* East Indiaman by a French privateer in the Bay of Bengal in 1800. Another tablet not far off, at Somerton, is to the memory of a twelve-year-old midshipman lost in 1811 in HMS *Hero*, seventy four guns, lost with all hands in a storm off the coast of Holland. Nevertheless the almost incessant wars of the eighteenth century, even the Revolutionary and Napoleonic Wars, seem to have inspired surprisingly few memorials either collective or individual.

The most productive period for individual memorials, before the Great War, was the nineteenth century, with its plentiful crop from the wars of the Empire. Captain John Bascombe, 5th Bengal Native Infantry, a native of Dorchester, 'died in the Khybur Pass, Upper India, January 24th, 1842, aged 34 Years. He fell in an action with the Affreedies whilst bravely struggling to convey the succour so much needed by the British forces in Affghanistan.' William Dalgleish Playfair, commemorated in the chapel of St Salvator's College, St Andrews, was a lieutenant in the 33rd Bengal Native Infantry 'who, on the 16th February 1846, in the memorable battle of Sobraon, while gallantly leading his company in the attack made by Sir Robert Dick's Division on the right of the Sikh intrenchments, fell mortally wounded in the 25th year of his age.' Thirty-three years later, as a nearby tablet records, Major John Cook VC., Bengal Staff Corps, 5th Goorkha Regiment, 'was mortally wounded in the attack on the Takht-i-Shahr Peak ... and died at Kabul on December 19 1879 in the thirty-seventh year of his age.'

In the building once occupied by the British consulate at Yokohama there is an elaborate memorial brass, put up by the British residents of the town, to two officers (including the captain) and nine marines and seamen of HMS *Euryalus*, to one marine and one seaman of HMS *Coquette*, and to one boy of HMS *Perseus*, all of whom 'fell in the naval action of Kagoshima' on 16th August 1863. The engagement followed on the murder of an

Englishman, Mr Richardson. The number of casualties, very heavy for a nineteenth-century battle against a non-European enemy, suggest that the Japanese, only thirteen years after they had been forced to open their country to foreigners, were already formidable.

These memorials of the nineteenth century and earlier commemorate professional soldiers and their officers. They remind us that soldiering was not a trade which many men willingly took up, and that although history is so largely made of war, the actual waging of it - the bloody end of the business - was in Britain, until 1914, the concern of comparatively few people, chiefly the men of regular regiments and 'Army families'. The number concerned with naval warfare was even smaller. Accordingly the old memorials testify to group loyalty and family piety, but not to widespread grief in the community at large. Our unsentimental ancestors were not unduly concerned with the fate of 'common soldiers'. 'How sleep the brave who sink to rest By all their country's wishes blest' was how an eighteenth-century poet put it, but an eighteenth-century lawyer probably came closer to most people's way of thinking when he remarked on 'the uncontrollable licentiousness of a brutal and insolent soldiery.'[1]

With the Great War memorials matters are far otherwise. From the Cenotaph to the dead of the British Empire in Whitehall down to tiny tablets with half-a-dozen names in village churches, they represent the community in the widest possible sense. So, no doubt, do the widespread memorials to the Great War in France and Germany, and, in the United States, the monuments to the Northern dead of the Civil War in Boston and, on the other side, the numerous memorials erected in Southern towns thirty or forty years after the Civil War ended. In Aspen, Colorado, there is a monument, put up in the eighteen-nineties, to the dead of both sides.

On the British memorials to the Great War the old affiliations of group and family still assert themselves, but with far wider scope. At the top of Highgate Hill in London four memorials were put up within two or three hundred yards of each other. One, in St Michael's church, carries the names of fifty-two parishioners. Outside the Congregational church twenty-seven names appear at the base of a cross. The family of a naval officer killed in a particularly hazardous and bloody raid on Zeebrugge in 1918 put up a lychgate to his memory, leading to the Congregational Church Hall. It carries also the names of thirteen members of a boys' organisation, connected with the church, which he had founded. Several of the names appear below the cross outside the church. The gate, at the time of writing this book, is neglected and forlorn. On the other side of Highgate High Street, outside Highgate School, there is a pair of tall memorial gates, a cross decorated with a sword and, on the wall of the school chapel, a tablet carved with 311 names, mostly of junior officers.

War memorials may be realistic, like the innumerable infantry privates up and down the country or the brutal stone howitzer with its crew at Hyde Park Corner. They may be elegantly allegorical in the clasical taste like the naked youth with a sword who, not far from the grim gunners round the howitzer, inappropriately commemorates men of the Machine Gun Corps. 'Saul', quotes the inscription, 'hath slain his thousands, and David his ten thousands.' That the memory of the dead could ever be forgotten or slighted was incomprehensible when the memorials were built. Many carry the confident biblical assertion 'Their name liveth for evermore', taken from verse 14 in the 45th chapter of Ecclesiasticus which begins 'Let us now praise famous men, and our fathers that begat us.' Below the list of names at Highgate School is the sombre adjuration 'Remember'.

The Great War memorials are overwhelmingly memorials to soldiers, especially infantry soldiers, for between 1914 and 1918 it was the army which was the great eater of men, and fighting by land knocked men down in hundreds of thousands. But not very many of the men whose names we read were professional soldiers. Here arises a matter, close to the heart of our subject, which will recur at intervals thoughout this book: British attitudes to the army and to military service generally. Conventional attitudes differed sharply, depending on whether service as an officer or in the ranks was being considered, but neither was likely to make a wide appeal as an occupation. Service in the ranks of the regular army had a very bad reputation indeed in early and mid-Victorian Britain, and as late as 1898 H. O. Arnold-Foster (1852-1909, Secretary of State for War 1903-05) wrote: 'No tradition is more deeply rooted in the minds of the poorer classes ... than that which represents enlistment as the last step in the downward career of a young man.'[2] At the other extreme of the social order service as an officer was an honourable and attractive occupation for gentlemen of good family who had no need to work for their living. 'To the young man who wants to enjoy himself,' wrote the grandson of a duke in 1897, 'to spend a few years agreeably in military companionship - to have an occupation - the British cavalry will be suited.'[3] This was precisely how the writer of those words - Winston Churchill - began his career, but his outlook was as foreign to the bulk of the middle class as the idea of enlistment was to the working class, and at the beginning of August 1914 the thought of becoming an army officer would have seemed very strange indeed to many of those who over the succeeding four years were to become so. Not, however, quite so strange as it would have appeared to their fathers. Attitudes to military service changed a good deal in the generation before 1914 and it is part of our purpose to consider the nature and effects of the change.

Every man who joined the army before the beginning of 1916 was a volunteer. So were many who joined later. Pressure of many kinds was brought to bear, but it had no force in law. Public opinion in Victorian and Edwardian Britain was invincibly set against the hated foreign notion of 'conscription':

> Go tell the world of Conscripts
> That Britain's Britain still;
> Go tell the world of Conscripts
> Our watchword's Freedom still.
> So let aggression's forc'd array
> Fill those it may with fears,
> We'll answer their conscription with
> *A Million Volunteers*[4].

The notion that compulsory service in arms was repugnant to British tradition was mistaken. No government, in the end, can do without it. For centuries there had been powers to draft landsmen into the militia - the 'old constitutional force' - for home defence and seamen into the fleet, and up to the end of the Revolutionary and Napoleonic Wars - known collectively until 1914 as 'the Great War' - they had been used without hesitation and without question. Then in the long peace which followed the press gang disappeared but militiamen were 'embodied' - that is, called out for full-time service - during the Crimean War (1854-6), the Indian Mutiny (1857-8) and, in large numbers, during the Boer War (1899-1902). They could not be sent overseas without their own consent, but 45,566 went to South Africa, where they were 'regarded as second-line troops of inferior quality'. The Victorian militia had become a part-time voluntary force with a hint of compulsion behind it. It was a useful source of recruits for the regular army, but a writer of the 1880's considered that any attempt at compulsion 'would, in the present state of public opinion, lead to determined resistance.'[5] No doubt he was right.

Militia service was not at all the same thing as conscription. First, it was for home service only unless the militiamen agreed to go overseas. Secondly, militia service was not universal. Those who were to serve by compulsion were chosen by ballot, and even at the height of the Napoleonic War anyone so chosen could legally provide a substitute, so that no one in the middle classes or above need serve unless he chose, for he had only to find some one who, for a consideration, would agree to serve in his place, and among the poor there was no shortage. 'Conscription', on the other hand, meant universal full-time compulsory military service, usually for a period of years, which was a very different matter. The justice of such a system, embracing all alike, made no appeal to the Victorians. What they saw and detested was the principle of compulsion. Liberals especially, with their suspicion of all things military, found the idea of conscription utterly unacceptable.

Before 1914 any British government which needed men for the regular army in peace or war had to bid against other employers. The bid was not strong. The pay of a private soldier in the infantry in 1914, after stoppages, came to 6s 8½d (about 33p) a week. Higher rates were offered in the cavalry, but even with a gorgeous scarlet tunic thrown in, as well as board and lodging, it was not easy for recruiting sergeants to make army life attractive. For infantry of the line they had to search low. 'It is this unalterable rule of voluntary service which fixes the quality and status of the men who constitute the rank and file', wrote T. H. S. Escott in 1879. 'These cannot ... be drawn from more than one source of supply ... the market for unskilled labour, in which alone the Government competes.'[6] The force of his observation shows in Irish recruiting figures. In 1851, just after the famine of the mid-1840's, Ireland, with 24 per cent of the population of the United Kingdom, provided 37 per cent of the men in the British army. Forty years later the proportions were down to 12 per cent of the population and 14 per cent of the men in the army.[7] Presumably conditions of life in Ireland had come more closely into line with conditions elsewhere in the United Kingdom.

'Every man', Dr Johnson is reported to have said, 'thinks meanly of himself for not having been a soldier.'[8] Perhaps, but the Victorians, like the men of Johnson's day, managed to live quite contentedly with their shame. The Crimean War and the Indian Mutiny prompted noisy patriotism, but the mid-Victorian was clear enough about the distinction between a soldier and a civilian. The civilian might join the Volunteers, and many did when a French threat appeared in the 1860's. That, however, was the equivalent of joining a club rather than joining the army, which was organised quite separately. The volunteer accepted a rather distant prospect of home defence, but war overseas was the regular soldier's business. That was what he was paid for, and in wartime the civilian's chief duty, apart from cheering the troops as they went overseas and as they came back again, was to pay out even more in taxation than usual. Income tax, invented to pay for war, should in theory have ceased when there was no war, and Gladstone hoped to do away with it. His hopes were dashed by the Crimean War. Income tax more than doubled, from 7d (under 3p) in the pound to 1s 4d (over 6p).[9]

Later, as imperialist enthusiasm grew, there were signs that this attitude was changing. Hugh Cunningham says that when war with Russia seemed likely in 1877-8 a number of Volunteer corps offered to go overseas. They were not accepted. During the fighting in Egypt in 1882 and again in 1885 volunteers did reach the theatre of war, though as specialists, not fighting troops. The men concerned were employees of the Post Office, and in 1885 railwaymen from Crewe went out as well.[10]

In the 1880's eagerness to serve the Empire in arms was more noticeable in the colonies than at home. During the excitement surrounding Wolseley's attempt to rescue General Gordon from Khartoum volunteer troops were offered from Canada; from Victoria, New South Wales, South Australia; from Fiji; from Perak. Gladstone, presiding with immense distaste over the whole affair, acknowledged that they 'proceeded from one and the same spirit of loyalty and attachment to the Throne and Empire.'[11]

Opinion at the War Office was against amateurs, but an offer of artillery from New South Wales was accepted. On 3rd March 1885 800 men and 224 horses, the privates paid at the unheard-of rate of 5s (25p) a day and higher ranks proportionately upward, left Sydney for the Sudan. Enthusiasm was immense. The day was declared a public holiday. At a banquet a fortnight later the Colonial Treasurer said:

> In sending military assistance to England in a foreign country we were perfectly well aware that we were straining the powers of local provisions made for our own defence, but we resolved that, as members of the Empire, we were defending ourselves and all most dear to us just as much in Egypt as if the common enemy menaced us in this Colony.(Cheers)

From that flight of fancy he went on to another:

> We have been changed ... from an insignificant, small, unknown (comparatively speaking) colony to the observed of all observers, to be the topic of every capital in Europe, the theme of every breakfast table in the world.(Applause) We have ceased to be a dependency. We have risen to the position of being recognised as a portion of the British Empire, that glorious Empire upon which the sun never sets.[12]

Gordon was dead before the Australians sailed and they were soon on their way home. Nevertheless, they had been under fire at Suakin and two had been wounded. For the first time a volunteer unit, raised specifically for service overseas, had joined British troops in action. For the first time, faint and far away, the drums of 1914 were beating.

Lord Augustus Loftus, Governor of New South Wales, addressing the troops at the port of embarkation, did not let the significance of the occasion pass unnoticed:

> For the first time in the great history of the British Empire, a distant Colony is sending, at its own cost, and completely equipped, a contingent of troops who have volunteered with an enthusiasm of which only we who have witnessed it can judge, to assist the Imperial Forces in a bitter struggle for the suppression of unspeakable cruelty and for the establishment of order and justice in a misgoverned country ... You will be greeted in Egypt by the hearty welcome of thousands of chivalrous soldiers who have never yet looked upon such an action as yours. The eyes of our gracious Queen will be bent upon your exertions, and in every part of the world where our flag floats, men, women, and children will eagerly read of your exploits and pray for your success. Soldiers! You will have the glorious privilege of helping to maintain the honour of the Empire.[13]

No doubt much to the relief of British generals, none of the other imperial wars of the 1880's and 1890's attracted volunteers in the same way as the attempt to rescue Gordon, which had an emotional charge of peculiar intensity assiduously worked up by the emerging mass media. Then, in the autumn of 1899, the two Boer republics of South Africa - the South African Republic and the Orange Free State - declared war on Great Britain. A situation arose which produced on a small scale something approaching a rehearsal of the volunteering enthusiasm of 1914.

II

In 1899, for the first time since the Crimean War, the Queen's enemies were white and might in a sense be described as European, though few of them had ever seen Europe and in outlook and background they were as African as the blacks whom they dominated, though in quite a different way. They were far more dangerous, being better armed and organised, than the general run of the British Empire's opponents, even the Afghans and the Sikhs.

'The modern Boer', said Conan Doyle in 1900, is 'the most formidable antagonist who ever crossed the path of Imperial Britain ... Napoleon and all his veterans ... never treated us so roughly as these hard-bitten farmers with their ancient theology and their inconveniently modern rifles.'[14] At the end of 1899 they beat three British generals in one week - 'Black Week', 10th - 16th December. The shock to the national self-esteem, then at its highest point of late-Victorian inflation, was immense.

The Boer War broke out in an explosion of enthusiasm. On the Stock Exchange, as the Boer ultimatum ran out on 11th October 1899, they unfurled the Royal Standard and the Union Flag in the Rhodesian market and then sang the National Anthem and 'Rule, Britannia'. 'The ordinary Londoner', remarked a caustic observer, 'nourished upon the placards of the evening papers, is never able to resist the temptation to indulge in a debauch of Jingoism', and he might have said the same of the people of other towns as well. When the First Army Corps embarked at Southampton there were said to be half-a-million people cheering the Queen and the generals, singing the National Anthem, loading the soldiers with little presents, exhorting them to ''urry up. Else it will all be over afore you get there.'[15]

In this atmosphere, somewhat sobered by Black Week, civilians in considerable numbers began to show eagerness for active service. This was something the military authorities weren't used to and didn't like. If men wanted to join the regular army on a normal engagement, well and good, but this new and strange desire, often afflicting men of far higher social standing than the ordinary private soldier, to scramble into uniform and then out of it again as soon as the fighting stopped, was a phenomenon which the Victorian military mind neither understood nor approved. There was 'no immediate prospect', according to the Under Secretary for War on 24th November 1899, 'of our being able to avail ourselves of the patriotic offers of the Volunteers.'[16]

War Office resistance to the idea of raising troops for war service only was weakened by the pressure of opinion generated by Black Week, but it was far from collapsing entirely. A strictly limited number of men, already on the strength of Volunteer units, was accepted for service overseas, but whole Volunteer units were not accepted and the men who were to go were mustered in 'active service companies' attached to regular battalions: sixty-six such companies, in all, were formed, and they are said to have 'created a good impression in the field'. In the atmosphere prevailing round the turn of 1899-1900 10,500 men were raised with the greatest ease and many more would have come if they had been allowed. 'The Volunteers,' says a contemporary account, 'impelled by the lust of glory and the love of country, stepped to the front. To them Honour was more than Falstaff's "word" - and its possession was not solely with those who had died.'[17]

It is doubtful whether 'active service companies' did much to satisfy anyone's 'lust for glory', but at the same time as they were forming another far more glamourous body of troops was being raised: the grandly titled 'Imperial Yeomanry'. Every recruit was expected to be able to ride and to shoot: a requirement which added a touch of class and, as Conan Doyle put it, 'appealed to the sporting instincts of our race'. It was expected, and at first the expectation may have been largely fulfilled, that the Imperial Yeomen would chiefly be countrymen led by officers from the gentry: a reflection of a social order, unsullied by industry, much admired by regular officers and romantically minded authors. As Conan Doyle explained in 1900:

> This singular and formidable force was drawn from every part of England and Scotland, with a contingent of hard-riding Irish fox-hunters. Noblemen and grooms rode knee to knee in the ranks, and the officers included many well-known country gentlemen and masters of hounds ... Many young men about town justified their existence for the first time. In a single club ... peculiarly dedicated to the *jeunesse dorée*, three hundred members rode to the wars.[18]

In the Empire overseas many volunteer units, chiefly mounted, were raised, to the accompaniment of patriotic rhapsody at home. In South Africa itself about 52,000 men enlisted but, being directly menaced by invasion, they were not in quite the same category as those from elsewhere. As in 1885 Australians and Canadians showed great forwardness, and there were recruits from other countries as well. Altogether about 49,000 volunteers arrived in South Africa from other British colonies and dependencies, representing about 11 per cent of the 448,000 troops deployed by Great Britain during the war.[19] They were all white. 'On broad grounds of policy', Erskine Childers observed in 1907, 'nobody will deny that, in a war between two white races, destined to live side by side in the midst of a vast coloured population, natives should be armed only in case of the last necessity.'[20] Some natives, nevertheless, were armed. Any the Boers caught, they killed.

Conan Doyle, surveying the scene in South Africa in 1900, when the war seemed all but over, was much gratified:

> All the scattered Anglo-Celtic race had sent their best blood to fight for the common cause ... For the British as for the German Empire [he was referring to the Franco-Prussian war of 1870-1] much virtue had come from the stress and strain of battle. To stand in the market square of Bloemfontein and to see the warrior types around you was to be assured of the future of the race. The middle-sized, square-set, weather-tanned, straw-bearded British regulars crowded the footpaths. There also one might see the hard-faced Canadians, the loose-limbed dashing Australians ... the dark New Zealanders ... the gallant sons of Tasmania, the gentlemen troopers of India and Ceylon, and everywhere the wild South African irregulars ... The man

who could ... doubt that the spirit of the race burned now as brightly as ever, must be devoid of judgment and sympathy. The real glories of the British race lie in the future, not in the past. The Empire walks with an uncertain tread but ... its weakness is that of waxing youth and not of waning age.[21]

One volunteer's war is described by Erskine Childers (1870-1922) in his highly successful book *In the Ranks of the CIV*, published in 1900. He was of good social standing, cousin to Hugh Childers (1827-1896) who had been Chancellor of the Exchequer from 1882 to 1885, but he enlisted as an artillery driver, right at the bottom of the military ladder, and spent his army career looking after two horses. But then the CIV - City Imperial Volunteers - were volunteers of a very special kind, raised in December 1899 at the expense of the Corporation of London, which voted £25,000 for the purpose. Seven other donors between them added £32,000 more.

The City took great pride in its Volunteers, most of whom came from the Honourable Artillery Company and other Volunteer units already in existence. They were organised partly as infantry, partly as gunners with twelve half-pounder Vickers-Maxim guns, very up-to-date, with experts from Vickers' works specially enlisted to look after them. After three weeks' drill the first 500 men left for South Africa. On 12th January 1900 each man was presented with the Freedom of the City. Then they all went to a farewell service in St Paul's Cathedral. 'The cheering was loud and long ... the address by the Dean was brief and manly.' After that they were entertained until midnight to a feast in the Inner Temple. The next morning they marched to Nine Elms and then went by train - cheering, cheering all the way - to Southampton, where the Lord Mayor and Sheriffs of London saw them off.[22] For those who were killed or died in South Africa, memorials were provided from regimental funds.

The CIV were never numerous - about 2,000 all told - and they were quite unlike the regular army, being mostly men of good education and social position, as were Erskine Childers himself and his friend Basil Williams (1867-1950), who became a professor of history. Childers and Williams were in the field for about eight months. Their unit marched a great deal, fired off a satisfactory quantity of ammunition, and lost one man - through sickness, not bullets. Childers regarded the whole episode very much as an exhilaratingly dangerous form of sport. 'We have enjoyed it', he wrote of his first experience of coming under fire, 'for it is the real thing at last.'[23] Would this fresh and innocent enthusiasm have survived longer service or bloodier fighting?

In June Roberts took Pretoria. The war, it was assumed, was as good as over, and most of the volunteers were sent home. The CIV reached England in October, to find the stations beflagged in their honour all along the line from Southampton to London and a heroes' welcome awaiting them there. Childers reflected rather guiltily on 'a dusty khaki figure still plodding the distant veldt - our friend and comrade, Atkins [Thomas Atkins, pet name for the regular soldier] who had done more and bloodier work than we, and who is not at the end of it yet.'[24]

He was not, indeed. The Boers, in defiance of the accepted usages of nineteenth-century warfare, fought a guerilla campaign until 1902, so that the last phase of the Boer War was also the longest. It was boring rather than dangerous for the British troops, bringing the unpleasant and well-publicised work of destroying Boer farms and herding women and children into 'concentration camps' - the first time the phrase was used - and it totally lacked glamour. It was not at all the kind of war which in 1899 had attracted Childers, Williams and others who had a 'lust for glory', but after they had gone home volunteers were still needed.

In February 1901 the Government took the remarkable step of raising the pay of the Imperial Yeomanry to colonial rates - 5s. a day, or almost five times as much as the pay of regular infantry. The flow of infantry volunteers dried up at once and the Imperial Yeomanry became attractive to many men who would not otherwise have considered enlisting. They came forward readily - 17,000 in the spring of 1901, 7,000 in the winter of 1901-2. The stipulated qualifications for recruits to the Imperial Yeomanry - riding and shooting - were not seriously tested and recruits were given no training at home and little, except by experience, abroad. As a consequence, though it was hardly their fault, they were of little use in the field and they were heavily criticised, being unfavourably compared with the men who had gone out earlier. 'Those were what I would call the men who went out through patriotism at the end of 1899 and the beginning of 1900,' said Sir Thomas Kelly-Kenny, a divisional commander, 'but as to the other lots of Yeomanry, and also the other lots of Colonials, for I do not think there is very much difference, I think we had to buy them, and rather dearly, too.'[25]

The service of non-regular troops in South Africa tended to confirm the prejudice of regulars against them. 'For three solid years', wrote Archibald Hurd in 1911, '... did our British Regulars see local corps dissolved and reconstituted; see Yeomanry and Volunteers and overseas Colonial corps sail away to great receptions in their homes; see them relieved in due course by fresh substitutes drawing more than four times the Regular pay for identical work less efficiently performed.'[26] As for the non-regulars themselves, their service in South Africa, neither over-long nor over-bloody, hardly gave them a true impression of the fearful potentialities of twentieth-century war. Most of them served for less than a year and the regulars did nearly all the heavy fighting. Nor were the non-regulars from the mother country very numerous - say 27,000 Volunteers and 37,000 Imperial Yeomanry, altogether about 0.76 per cent of the 8.4 million men of military age (between twenty and fifty years old) in the United Kingdom. Those who served were generally admired, but those who stayed at home were not made to feel intolerably ashamed.

The raising of non-regular troops for South Africa, though an inadequate foretaste of the events of 1914, represented a major change in British attitudes, at home and in the colonies, to military service overseas. It was no longer eccentric for a civilian, in time of war, to become a temporary soldier. On the contrary, it was admirable. Formerly it had been entirely respectable for an able-bodied man to stay at home while the regulars fought overseas. Nothing else, indeed, was expected of him. After the Boer War, that was no longer true.

By 1914 the change in attitude had gone much further: so much further that within two months of the outbreak of war, without any form of legal compulsion but in an atmosphere of intense patriotic fervour, over three-quarters of a million men had joined the army, adding their strength to that of the quarter of a million already in the Territorial Force which had replaced the old Volunteers. Eventually more than $2\frac{1}{2}$ million joined the army in the United Kingdom before the first Military Service Act came into force at the beginning of 1916, and from the white population of the Empire came another 1.7 million.

How was this possible in Britain in 1914? How did it come about that men in millions could be persuaded to volunteer in a society which - in often-proclaimed contrast to German attitudes - prided itself on having no taint of militarism? The nation's general tone of opinion, its system of values and its conventional attitudes were set very largely by members of the upper middle class who, with their allies further up the social scale, had become dominant in British society during the nineteenth century, and they provided the leadership, social, political and military, under which the nation went to war. They are considered in rather more detail in Chapter Seven.

This book, accordingly, is very largely an examination of the development of upper-middle-class opinions and attitudes. This is very far from saying that those in power imposed their views upon an unwilling proletariat. There is, on the contrary, every indication that these views, or some approximation to them, were accepted much lower down the social scale. Whatever else the Great War may have been, it was in its early stages an extremely popular war - even perhaps in some obscure way a wanted war - and it was in high spirits, not sullenly, that Kitchener's armies went singing on their way to Ypres, to Gallipolli, to Loos, and to the Somme.

CHAPTER TWO

On war: Clausewitz, Darwin,
Henty and others

Kitchener's armies marched away to war of a kind that no one had seen before; war of a kind that some people said would never break out; war that nearly everyone expected would move fast to a thrilling climax and be over in a matter of months. To a generation that has cause to regard war as unmitigated catastrophe it comes as a shock to find a sensitive, highly educated, highly sophisticated poet - Rupert Brooke - writing, on his way to Gallipoli early in 1915: 'I've never been so happy in my life, I think'. Another young man of very different birth and education, under orders as a private soldier for France, wrote a month or so later: 'Roll on to-morrow, and the final journey that will take me to adventure!'[1] These eager volunteers had no means of knowing what lay ahead, for there had never yet been a war between the most powerful states of Europe, disposing of all the resources of modern industrial society, and few had guessed at what the true nature of such a clash would be.

How then did the British in 1914 look upon war? What form did they expect the conflict with Germany to take? In considering these questions, as in considering others throughout the book, we shall also be considering how opinion was formed and how those who formed it reached the public mind. We shall be looking, in short, at the working of the machinery by which an immense flood of material from journalists, illustrators ('our artist at the front'), novelists, writers for boys, musicians and song-writers was poured upon the pre-war public. It will be well to begin by considering what that machinery was, for without it the nation could hardly have reached the state of mind in which war was greeted with such enthusiasm in 1914.

For thirty-five years or so before 1914 the modern industry of mass communication was beginning to take shape, greatly facilitated by technical developments such as the development of railways and telegraph systems and of cheap and plentiful printing paper. During the 1880's and 1890's three young men were leading the way in showing that a large and profitable business could be founded on selling periodicals designed for a reading public which, with the general rise in real wages in late Victorian Britain, could afford in large numbers to pay for them, just as the same class of people could afford Lever's Sunlight Soap, Cadbury's cocoa, Lipton's tea, ready-made clothes, cheap furniture. These people had an enormous appetite for information, as George Newnes (1851-1910) was the first to demonstrate with *Tit-Bits* in 1881. Alfred Harmsworth (1865-1922), later Lord Northcliffe, followed Newnes into the same market with *Answers to Correspondents*, generally known as *Answers*, in 1888. In 1890 C. A. Pearson

(1866-1921) launched *Pearson's Weekly*. These were the leaders, but they had many competitors. They built on their success, especially Harmsworth, by multiplying the number of their publications. By 1891 Newnes was selling 500,000 copies of *Tit-Bits* a week and in the same year an accountant certified that the weekly net sales of copies of all Harmsworth publications totalled more than a million.[2] In 1896 Harmsworth brought out the *Daily Mail* , priced at a halfpenny and aimed at a mass circulation. In 1900 it reached, though it did not hold, a circulation of a million, and in the years between 1900 and 1914 its circulation fluctuated round three-quarters of a million, very much more than that of any other daily paper.[3]

The educated classes had their political and literary reviews, *Punch*, *The Times*, and a wide range of other periodicals and newspapers. They were scornful of the style and content of the mass-market periodicals, perhaps the more so because they were highly profitable and unashamedly run for profit rather than with the political and cultural aims of the older journalism. The early successes - *Tit-Bits*, *Answers*, *Comic Cuts* and the rest - were crude, exceedingly simple, and relied a great deal on competitions and other devices for boosting their circulation, but alongside them periodicals of much greater sophistication - *Review of Reviews*, for example, in 1890, and *The Strand Magazine* in 1891 - began to appear from the same publishing houses.

As well as periodicals, 'part works' became very numerous, being sold over a period in numerous parts intended eventually to be bound together in a volume or, more likely, a series of volumes. Between 1897 and the outbreak of the Great War Harmsworths published at least seventeen part-works including *Sixty Years a Queen* (1897) in ten sixpenny ($2\frac{1}{2}p$) parts, forty eight parts of *Everywoman's Encyclopaedia* in 1910, ten parts of *Nelson and his Times*, two works on the Boer War in seventy-two parts altogether, and the *Harmsworth Self-Educator* (1905) in forty-eight parts. Many other publishers were in the same market. Cassells were among the most prolific. They published, for instance, an *Illustrated History of the Boer War* in thirty fortnightly parts at 6d each. In this way people who would be unwilling to lay out several shillings at a time for a book or books found themselves able to acquire works on an immense variety of subjects, authoritatively written and attractively presented, for a shilling ($5p$) or so a month.

The publishing revolution which began in the 1880's set in motion processes by which information and ideas could penetrate more rapidly, widely and deeply in society than ever before. There was a great deal of simplification, even distortion, and there was also triviality, but a mind-broadening engine of great power had come into action, and as the decades passed its power increased. Between 1881 and 1911 the number of authors, editors and journalists in England and Wales recorded in the census rose by more than 300 per cent from 3,434 to 13,786.[4] The printed word was not equalled as a medium for influencing opinion or imparting information until the rise, first, of 'wireless' and later of televison.

The influence of the printed word was not confined to newspapers and periodicals. There was an expanding book trade, including trade in books aimed at the children's market. In boys' adventure stories, in school stories, in many works of popularisation - particularly those dealing with the Empire and the armed forces - ideas of war, of patriotism and of duty were fed into young minds during the years in which the soldiers of the Great War grew up. Works of this type were more explicitly didactic than those aimed at grown-up audiences. Their authors intended to pass on a message, and they did.

II

We turn now from the machinery for conveying ideas to the ideas themselves, addressing ourselves first to general theoretical notions of the nature of war. Starting in the upper intellectual atmosphere, let us glance at two nineteenth-century thinkers, neither likely to be familiar to ordinary Englishmen, unless indirectly and superficially, and far removed from each other in subject-matter. One is Karl von Clausewitz (1780-1831), a Prussian general who served against Napoleon, and the other is Charles Darwin (1809-1882), who came of a numerous family at the centre of the high-Victorian 'intellectual aristocracy' (see p. 129 below) of liberal Britain.

Clausewitz's book *On War*, first published in 1832, was immensely influential, probably because its message was shocking and at the same time welcome to those in nineteenth-century Europe who had an interest in making war respectable. Early in his first volume, with the famous pronouncement 'war is the continuation of policy by other means', Clausewitz makes it clear that he regards war as a normal part of the mechanics of politics. The discussion proceeds from that point of view, on the underlying assumption that governments have a right to make war which they may exercise without incurring moral censure. War, Clausewitz says, is compatible with civilisation: 'The greatest names ... that have been renowned in War belong strictly to episodes of higher culture.' War satisfies 'the soul's longing for honour and renown.' War, in short, 'is part of the intercourse of the human race.'[5]

There remained a feeling of moral *malaise*. In an age when people set great store by scientific laws it was comforting to find that Darwin's theory of natural selection, interpreted as 'the survival of the fittest', could be used to show that the stronger nations would always overwhelm the weaker, indicating that the stronger nations were the best. War, beastly though it might be, thus worked with other agencies of evolution for the general good of the human race.

'What Darwin accomplished for Biology generally Clausewitz did for the Life-History of Nations nearly half a century before him', wrote Colonel F. N. Maude (1854-1933), an intellectual soldier, in 1908, 'for both have proved the existence of the same law in each case, viz "The survival of the fittest" - "the fittest" not being necessarily synonymous with the ethically "best".'[6] Colonel Maude's somewhat suspect reasoning shows how far an intelligent man may go in finding reasons for believing what he wants to believe. There were plenty like him, especially among those anxious to find not only a good political case but also a good ethical case for war.

If war was part of the divinely ordained process of evolution, it was a short step to the asssertion that making war might itself be a virtuous activity highly approved, in selected cases, by that wrathful deity the Lord of Hosts. In Britain there was an unspoken assumption, unconnected with Darwin or Clausewitz, that He had ceased to be Hebrew and had taken British nationality, or at any rate was on our side: as Kipling put it:

> For the Lord our God Most High,
> He hath made the deep as dry,
> He hath smote for us a pathway to the ends of all the Earth.[7]

A strong Lord-of-Hosts man who was also an exponent of the 'ruthless, inexorable ... law of the survival of the fittest' was H. F. Wyatt(d. 1925), an Oxford man, the son of a clergyman, Honorary Secretary of the Navy League in 1905, and a tireless propagandist. *'God's Test by War'*, published as an article in 1911 and expanded into a book in 1912, is a fair specimen of a numerous class of literature. It shows what happened when evolutionary theory was interpreted in the light of warlike and muscular Christianity with a strong puritan flavour.[8]

'War is the supreme instrument', Wyatt announces, of the law of the survival of the fittest, 'and of war, in the long passage of the centuries, the deciding factor is the soul.'[9] Having pointed out that defeat in war follows from naval and military inefficiency, which is 'the inevitable sequel to moral decay', he moves to stirring rhetoric:

> The Lord of Hosts has made righteousness the path to victory ... Not necessarily in any given case, but absolutely certainly in the majority of cases, the triumph of the victor has been the triumph of the nobler soul of man. Though to this rule history may furnish a thousand exceptions;

though in history war has been made a thousand times over the instrument of cruel oppression and diabolical wrong, yet in that great majority of instances which determines general results the issue of war has made for the ethical advantage of mankind. It must have been so; it could not be otherwise, because ethical quality has tended always to produce military efficiency.[10]

This startling train of reasoning leads to a conclusion no less startling:

Preparation for war is the enemy of sloth. Preparation for war is the dissolvent of apathy. Victory is the prize not alone of present self-sacrifice and present energy, but also of previous self-sacrifice and previous energy. Briefly, victory is the crown of moral quality, and therefore, while nations wage war on one another, the 'survival of the fittest' means the survival of the ethically best ...

This was further even than Colonel Maude had been prepared to go, but Wyatt buttressed his assertion with two examples from history: the English fourteenth-century archers who 'shot death into the ranks of the chivalry of France' and 'the Puritan mariners of our seaports' who 'in Elizabethan days ... laid the foundations of empire by vindicating at the cannon's mouth the freedom of the seas.' 'Was not the prowess of those good English yeomen', he asked, 'the direct product of a national life superior in its ... moral quality to that of the French, or perhaps of any other European people of the day?', and then: 'was there not in those men [the Puritan mariners] moral quality ... of a kind higher than that of the Spaniard whom they vanquished?'[11] Well, perhaps, but had Wyatt tried asking a Frenchman or a Spaniard?

The contention that the survival of the fittest meant also the survival of the ethically best percolated into fiction. 'Saki' (H. H. Munro, 1870-1916) published early in 1914 *When William Came*, a cautionary account, examined at greater length in Chapter Four, of a German conquest of Britain. The Germans win not only because they are better prepared but because they are morally superior.

Maud Diver, who died in 1945, was the daugher of an army officer and the wife of another. She had therefore something of a family interest in military virtue, and in the course of her long and successful literary career war and soldiering, seen as a school of manly excellence, is among her favourite themes. It is central to her first successful novel, *Captain Desmond, VC* (1907), and to its sequel *Desmond's Daughter*, published in 1916 but 'conceived and partially written before the war.' The hero of *Desmond's Daughter*, Vincent Leigh, is an army officer's son, destined himself for the army. He dislikes Sandhurst so much that he is on the point of forsaking it for Oxford and a literary career. He is deterred from this unworthy course by talking to a retired officer of the Indian Army:

> "I suppose you've done a good deal of fighting yourself?"[Leigh] asked.
> "A fair amount, here and there. Why?"
> "Didn't something inside you always shrink, always rebel, at the hideousness - the brutality?"
> "Yes, always."
> "And yet - you uphold war?"
> "Yes. As a last resort, I uphold war," Colonel Wyndham replied with his grave smile. "That sounds paradoxical; but war is the great paradox, the greatest in human history. It spells horror, but it also spells heroism, which is possibly what commends it to most healthy-minded men ... Call it which you like, a terrible medicine or an intermittent eruption of evil; it is still ... the Great Flail that threshes the wheat from the chaff. So, in the long run, it makes for the ethical advance of the race."[12]

One attraction of this line of thought was that it offered the practising Christian a solution to the problem of reconciling the waging of war with his religious convictions. Quakers simply held that it was un-Christian to take any part in warfare, but other believers held deep-rooted notions of honourable conduct to which uncompromising pacificism was repugnant. If, as Wyatt and others claimed, war was part of God's plan for the ethical improvement of mankind, their difficulty disappeared, for pacifism was a wrong-headed delusion and war service became legitimate. 'It is lawful for Christian men', Article XXVII of the Church of England's Articles of Religion declares, 'at the commandment of the Magistrate, to wear weapons, and serve in the wars.'

The Christian conscience, nevertheless, called some remarkable mental gymnastics into play. Fr H. I. D. Ryder, a theologian at Brompton Oratory in London, wrote an article in 1899 on the ethics of war. He took the text 'If my kingdom were of this world verily would my servants have fought, so that I should not be delivered into the hands of the Jews' (John xviii 36). From it he argued that if an earthly kingdom were justifiable - 'as even Quakers admit that it is' - then there was 'Scripture warranty to fight for it.' 'The Scripture of both Testaments', he went on, 'is full of the imagery of war, which would surely never be the case were war essentially criminal.' It seems a questionable argument.

In considering the perennial problem of what constitutes a just war, Ryder put forward a contention which might have startled a good many people. A defensive war, if hopeless, would not be just, but an offensive war, launched to prevent a threatened attack, might be. 'Must we', he asked, 'await the attack of a wild beast before we fire?' He was in no doubt, in an imperialist age, of the rights of 'pioneers of civilisation representing the great European Powers' to open up countries in the name of progress. The rights of primitive peoples he scornfully dismissed. 'I cannot pretend', he wrote, 'that savages, who do but abrade the earth like so many fowl, have established any exclusive and inviolable right to possession.'

Ryder did not claim that a state, in making war, was necessarily carrying forward any great ethical principle. In this he differed from the Darwinians. 'It is humiliating but certainly true', he wrote, '... that nations may hardly pretend to more than the morality of the average schoolboy, who must win and keep his place in public estimation by showing his readiness to fight for it.'[13] More realistic than many liberals, he recognised that states cannot be expected to act on the same Christian principles as individuals.

The general sentiment of the day accepted physical violence, as it had always been accepted in the past, as part of the natural order, and people were ready to admire those who had recourse to it in a good cause, from a boy defending a bully's victim to General Gordon doing rather the same thing on a larger scale at Khartoum. War had its place in this scheme of things, and if Christianity said otherwise, so much the worse for Christianity. Many Victorians solved the problem by thinking of religion in terms of the Church Militant, as the stirring martial imagery of popular hymns bears witness. 'Fight the good fight', by the Rev. Dr John Monsell (1811-75) is an adaptation of 2 Timothy iv 7: 'I have fought a good fight, I have finished my course, I have kept the faith.' Others, also at a greater or less distance from specified texts, include 'Conquering kings their titles take' (John Chandler, 1806-76), 'Soldiers of Christ arise', one of 6,000 hymns by Charles Wesley (1707-88) and, perhaps most popular of all, 'Onward, Christian Soldiers' by the Rev. Sabine Baring-Gould (1834-1924), set to music by Sir Arthur Sullivan (1842-1900). Militant religion of this kind had a special attraction for evangelicals within the Church of England and dissenters outside it, heirs to the puritans who believed in holding a bible in one hand and a sword in the other. That tradition was strong in Victorian England and 'puritan' was a term of admiration, not abuse.

There was a widespread feeling that Christian pacifism was unacceptable. Sir Henry Newbolt (1862-1938) who, like Kipling, frequently put his own views into mouths of an earlier age, makes one of his fictional characters say of the Black Prince (1330-76):

... if any man was ever born a Christian, he was. But on the point of war, he no more accepts the Church's view of Christianity than ... any other Englishman who is honest with himself. He does not believe that war is always unlawful; he knows that all existence is a struggle [had the Black Prince read Darwin?], that we love fighting because it is the savour of life itself, and that in this world of forces everything must depend on force in the last resort.[14]

There was a strong belief, not without some foundation in fact, that warfare between European powers in the nineteenth or twentieth century would be 'civilised warfare'. The phrase was used, quite without irony, by authors as different as Victorian contributors to *The Nineteenth Century* and the writer of the British Army's *Textbook of Small Arms* who, in discussing the stopping power of 'specially made "expanding" bullets', said in 1929: 'these were used against savages and fanatics. But in civilized warfare these are expressly ruled out ...'.[15] Attacks on civilians were not contemplated, and all the numerous mid-century European wars - the Crimean War, the war of 1859 in Italy, Bismarck's wars in the 1860's, the Franco-Prussian War of 1870-1 - were fought on the principle that fighting was bloody but ferocity was selective. There was the corollary that civilians were not permitted to attack troops, and *francs tireurs* were liable to be shot if taken.

'Under the touch of civilisation', wrote Fr Ryder, 'war has lost some of its most offensive features. The condition of non-combatants is immensely relieved, and we may regard the sack which gave defenceless women and children to the mercy of a maddened soldiery, and the bombardment of unfortified towns and harbours, as henceforth excluded from the casualties of civilised warfare.' At the first meeting of the Society of Telegraph Engineers in 1873 a reference by a naval officer (Captain Dawson) to 'the uncivilised purposes of civilised war' was considered by his audience to be in rather poor taste.[16]

Admiral Fisher (1841-1920) would have understood Captain Dawson. At The Hague Conference of 1899, set up by the Czar to consider disarmament, he shocked the other delegates by predicting aerial bombardment and poison gas, but then 'Jacky' was a well-known eccentric. When in 1913 he suggested that German submarines might attack British merchant ships the First Lord of the Admiralty, Winston Churchill, replied that he did not believe this would ever be done by any civilised power.[17]

The conduct of the Boer War seemed to justify belief in 'civilised warfare'. The Boers, though fiercely set on maintaining their independence, fought within the rules, except when blacks were taken in arms. The British, though aggressively imperialist, had traditions of sportsmanship which they took very seriously. The fighting men did not hate one another and the wounded could safely be left for the other side to look after. Sir Ian Hamilton (1853-1947) said in 1903 that 'both sides were far more anxious to obtain a surrender than to kill or wound their adversaries.'[18] A subaltern in the field, on the other hand, wrote to his father: 'The more Boers we can wipe out now the better for the future.'[19] The same officer, looking back in 1937 on what he had by then come to think of as 'the last of the gentlemen's wars', said: 'as wars go, the war in South Africa was probably the most humane ever fought.'[20] No doubt distance lent enchantment to the view, but he may have been right, even allowing for the concentration camps in which many Boer women and children died after their farms had been burnt. Guerilla campaigns, as we know only too well to-day, are not gentlemanly, though the guerilla war fought by the Boers was less ungentlemanly than many since.

It was generally believed, before 1914, that a war between great powers would be short. John Gooch reminds us that both Sir Charles Dilke in 1887 and I. S. Bloch, a Polish economist and banker in 1899, recognising the power of the defence, with magazine rifles, in late nineteenth-century warfare, had forecast long wars of stalemate.[21] In general, however, the accepted models seem to have been Bismarck's wars of swift movement, culminating in the campaign of 1870-1 against France. The contrary example of the American Civil War, in many ways more compelling, seems to have been given very little weight. Perhaps it was too far away, but slightly nearer home more attention might have been paid to the siege of Plevna, where the Russians were held up for 143 days in 1877, and to some of the battles in South Africa, where the Boers several times demonstrated the power of determined riflemen to hold up frontal attacks on entrenched positions.

Sidney Lowe (1857-1932), an influential journalist, referred in 1898 to 'the rare and brief, if terrible, wars of modern times.' The American Admiral A. T. Mahan (1840-1914), one of the most widely respected strategic theorists of his day, remarked soothingly: 'when a convulsion does come, it passes rapidly, leaving the ordinary course of events to resume sooner, and therefore more rapidly.[22] With observations such as these passing for informed comment, how was the ordinary man to judge the probable length of the Great War when it broke out?

This brief survey suggests that in Britain before 1914 there was a considerable body of opinion which, far from regarding war as thoroughly evil, was prepared to make a case for it as a necessary part of the evolutionary process and even as something good in itself. Moreover in the civilised world of the late nineteenth and early twentieth centuries warfare itself, it was expected, would be civilised - and brief. The writers who were putting these ideas about were not representing extreme groups at odds with respectable opinion. On the contrary, they had periodicals such as *The Nineteenth Century* offering a platform and their books readily found publishers.

Writing of the kind so far considered would not have reached directly a wide readership. But the readership it did reach was influential in forming opinion and ideas once set afloat could spread downwards and outwards, through the channels already indicated, far beyond their origins, mingling on the way with traditional patriotism and the rising imperialism discussed in the next chapter, and becoming eventually part of the common stock of received ideas, part of the common culture. Among those who popularised notions of war on a lower intellectual level than those so far examined were the writers of boys' adventure stories and the war correspondents of British newpapers. The two groups had a large public for their views. They overlapped in the person of G. A. Henty (1832-1902).

III

Henty, still well known today and still in print as a boys' writer, in his own time was very active as a war correspondent. When the Crimean War broke out in 1854 he was at Gonville and Caius College Cambridge. He left the university without a degree in order to serve in the Crimea with the Purveyor's Department. He was invalided home, but in 1859 he was well enough to be sent to Italy 'charged with the task of organising the hospitals of the Italian Legion' in the war with Austria which was then going on.[23] Soon after that campaign he left government service to become a war correspondent. In that capacity he was in Italy again in 1866; in Abyssinia (Ethiopia) in 1867-8; in Paris in 1870-1, including the period of the Commune; in Ashanti with Wolseley in 1873-4; in Spain for one of the Carlist wars in 1874; and in the Balkans for the Turco-Serbian war of 1876.

Henty was thus well qualified to provide a military or naval setting for the boys' adventure stories which he started to write in 1868. Over the next thirty years or so he ranged over a period from the Punic Wars to Roberts's advance on Pretoria in 1900. His friend and biographer George Manville Fenn (1831-1909), himself a boys' writer, says:

> it speedily dawned upon him that there is nothing a boy likes better than a good description of a fight - with fisticuffs not objected to against some school tyrant - and here, in his descriptions, the writer was thoroughly at home ... His boys were fighting boys, very manly, full, as he termed it, of pluck ... not so much boys as men, saving ... that he kept them to boy life,

and never made his works sickly by the introduction of ... the tender passion. "No," he said, "I never touch on love interest. Once I ventured to make a boy of twelve kiss a little girl of eleven, and I received a very indignant letter from a dissenting minister."[24]

Boys' writers were marvellously prolific. W. H. G. Kingston (1814-80) is credited with 'more than a hundred' boys' books between 1850 and his death, as well as editorial work. R. M. Ballantyne (1825-94) produced more than eighty titles in forty years. Dr Gordon Stables MD RN (1849-1910) contributed freely, from 1880 onward, to *The Boy's Own Paper,* as well as writing books. Henty's output ran to about seventy books for boys as well as ten adult novels. He also wrote *March to Magdala* and *March to Coomassie,* dealing with his experiences as a war correspondent. A writer of a younger generation, P. F. Westerman (1876-1959), claimed 'well over 150 boys' books'. He published *A Lad of Grit* in 1908 and during the Second World War was still turning out three titles a year. In his last years he slowed down a little.[25]

This immense output was not all on warlike themes, but the authors' favourite virtues were essentially military. Moreover it is often stated or implied that war is fun: as, for instance, by Gordon Stables in *By Sea and Land: A Story of the Blue and the Scarlet:* 'There was a smile on every face, which the prospect of a little fighting never fails to call forth in every class of sailor.'[26] It is taken for granted that healthy-minded boys of all ages enjoy fighting, for manliness thrives on fighting and manliness (in 1900 the Warden of Merton College Oxford went so far as to say: 'I like to see young women manly')[27] ranks high among the virtues. This was what the authors of boys' books continually told their readers and it is presumably what their readers wanted to hear. Writing of the great success of Henty's stories Manville Fenn said:

> They are essentially manly and he used to say that he wanted his boys to be bold, straightforward and ready to play a young man's part, not to be milksops. He had a horror of a lad who displayed any weak emotion and shrank from shedding blood, or winced at any encounter.[28]

Many stories first reached their readers as serials in the boys' magazines of the day, which also carried short stories and much else. *The Boys' Own Paper* was launched in 1879. Among its competitors was *Young England,* launched about a year earlier, *Chums* (1892) and Newnes's *The Captain* (1899).[29] All these and others appeared not only as weeklies but as stoutly bound, attractive annuals with a much longer reading life.

Some publishers issued collections of short stories in the same format - large books with coloured covers and plentiful illustrations, often on cheap paper to keep the price down. *Peril and Patriotism* (Cassell, 1901) shows on its cover a mounted white man throttling a savage, on foot but armed with a rifle. Its frontispiece, 'Back to back at Maiwand', illustrates a disastrous battle of the Second Afghan War (1878-80). John F. Shaw's *At Duty's Call on Land and Sea* (c. 1905) has a cover on which a warship's steam picket boat, in Chinese waters, is speeding to the rescue of a drowning man.

As well as these collections of fiction there was a large output of well-produced books of non-fiction, aimed at schoolchildren though not intended as formal textbooks. Some, such as Ward, Lock's *Wonder Book of Empire* and *Wonder Book of Soldiers,* come very close to our subject and are discussed below (pp. 40,58). The boys' magazines circulated at all social levels, the books, perhaps, rather among the middle classes than lower, but all were part of the great expansion of publishing from about 1880 onward and were likely to be familiar to many of the boys who became the men of Kitchener's armies.

Probably the principal route by which books, as distinct from magazines, reached boys' hands was as presents or prizes. The numerous prizes given in Board schools and in Sunday schools must have been very important in getting books circulated at the lower end of the social scale. Publishers cultivated the prize market, and at the back of their books they would print lists of titles, many in cheap editions, aimed specifically at those who chose prizes. 'Our boys' instructors', said G. M. Fenn, 'in conning the publishers' lists, would come upon some famous name for the hero of the story and exclaim "Ha! History; that's safe." In this way Henty [and Fenn himself and many others] taught more lasting history to boys than all the schoolmasters of his generation.'[30] Provided, of course, that those who received the prizes read them: not always a safe assumption, to judge by the number of copies in mint condition, or near it, that turn up in second-hand bookshops to-day.

Besides authors whose reputations rested chiefly on their work for boys there were others, some very well known, who produced, among other works, warlike tales aimed at boys or likely to appeal to them. Charles Kingsley's *Westward Ho!* (1855), a tale of adventure on the Spanish Main celebrating the militancy of Elizabethan protestantism, was the only book of its kind that Kingsley wrote, but it is probably unique among books in having had a town named after it. Conan Doyle wrote idealised tales of the Hundred Years War: *The White Company* and *Sir Nigel.* He also published two collections, in 1896 and 1903, of tales of a fictitious *French* hero, semi-heroic, semi-comic, of the Napoleonic wars, Brigadier Gerard, for which he took very great care to make his military detail accurate. He was very proud of his historical novels, saying of the two medieval tales, in 1924: 'I believe that if I had never touched [Sherlock] Holmes ... my position in literture would ... be a more commanding one.'[31]

Sir Henry Newbolt showed the same infatuation with military themes. He burst unwisely into prose, in *The Old Country* (1906) and *The Book of the Happy Warrior* (1917), with highly romanticised visions of fourteenth-century warfare and of the institution of chivalry, to which by spectacular sleight of historical hand he traced the origins of the Victorian public-school system (p. 93 below). In 1902 A. E. Mason (1865-1948), a profilic and highly accomplished novelist, published *The Four Feathers,* a tale of high adventure which takes full advantage of Kitchener's reconquest of the Sudan some four years earlier.

For impressions of war the Victorian and Edwardian public did not need to rely entirely on fiction. Somewhere in the world the real thing was always happening, and for the first time there was something like a mass market for reports of it, which could get into print very much faster than at any time in the past. W. H. Russell, for instance, travelling through Belgium from North-Eastern France by train and crossing the Channel by steamer, could bring an account of the battle of Sedan to London, immediately after it had been fought, and then go back to the Prussian army, all between 4th and 7th September 1870.[32] Travel by train and steamship, as this example shows, was rapid, the telegraph had a very long reach, and censorship as the twentieth century has come to understand it hardly existed, although it was being complained of as early as 1890.[33] As a result, the late nineteenth and early twentieth century became the first great age of the war correspondent, with the war artist, and from the Crimea onward the war photographer, alongside him.

War correspondents were not numerous. Henty, in the 1890's, thought only a dozen or so were employed regularly by British newspapers.[34] John Dawson, advising on journalism as a career, and taking a prosaically unheroic view of the journalist's trade, said: 'A young man who cares to qualify himself for the post of war correspondent will find that ... there is never likely to be many competitors, simply because of the dangers that necessarily attend the calling.'[35] Temporary correspondents, like the young Winston Churchill, would be engaged whenever fighting on any scale broke out. Success depended on the individual correspondent's enterprise and on his relationship with commanders in the field. W. H. Russell, during the campaign of 1870, was attached to the headquarters of the army of the Crown Prince of Prussia and was received in very high circles indeed. Most commanders were wary of correspondents and there are indications in Russell's diary that his friends in high places were careful to see that he did not penetrate inconveniently far into military secrets. Wolseley had a thoroughly modern awareness of the value of publicity, but he called war correspondents 'the curse of modern armies', and Kitchener was extremely hostile, though even he could not prevent his campaigns from being very frankly reported.

War correspondents' backgrounds covered the whole social landscape. W. H. Russell (1819-1907) came of Irish gentry. G. A. Henty's father was a mining engineer, and Henty himself spent some time in mining. Archibald Forbes (1838-1900), son of a Scottish minister, went to Aberdeen University, then heard a course of lectures by Russell and took a very unusual course for a middle-class man: he enlisted in the Royal Dragoons, with whom he served for five years in the early 1860's, and while he was still a trooper he was writing for the *Morning Star* and the *Cornhill Magazine*.[36] G. W. Steevens (1869-1900) 'came of good, sound, middle-class stock, was born in a London suburb', spoke with a cockney accent, and had a brilliant academic career at school and at Oxford before going into journalism.[37] W. L. S. Churchill, an enormously ambitious cavalry subaltern from a ducal family, could get Lord Kitchener's hostility to himself overridden by a word from a judge's wife, who was a friend of the family, to the Adjutant-General.[38] Edgar Wallace (1875-1932), brought up by a Billingsgate fish porter and his wife, reached journalism, as Forbes did, though under very different circumstances, from the ranks of the regular army.[39]

The war correspondents' approach to their job was workmanlike. Their trade was the soldier's trade, war. They had no qualms about its morality and they wanted to see the day's work efficiently done, so they were freely critical. Russell's attack on military maladministration during the Crimean War eventually affected the whole machinery of government. Forbes, almost equally influential, writing in the 1880's, compared British tactical training unfavourably with German and came close to calling it cowardly, supporting his remarks with observations on the battle of Tel-el-Kebir (1882), the most admired victory of the most admired general of the day, Sir Garnet Wolseley, created a baron for his conduct of the very campaign of which Tel-el-Kebir was the centrepiece.[40] G. W. Steevens deflated the romanticism of the charge of the 21st Lancers at Omdurman with the comment 'the blunders of British cavalry are the fertile seed of British glory.'[41] Churchill, a junior officer in his twenties, discussed the conduct of the Boer War by Buller and other generals.[42] No wonder Forbes once wrote: 'Were I a general, and had I an independent command in war offered me, I should accept it only on condition that I should have the charter to shoot every war correspondent found within fifty miles of my headquarters.'[43]

'Is not war all brutal?' Forbes asked rhetorically.[44] 'War, disguise it as you may,' wrote Churchill, 'is but a dirty, shoddy business which only a fool would play at.'[45] 'It was not a battle,' G. W. Steevens wrote of Omdurman, 'but an execution.'[46] In these phrases the war correspondent is a realist, well aware of the beastliness which he is observing. Churchill was eloquent on the horrors of the field of Omdurman. 'In a space not exceeding a hundred yards square more than four hundred corpses lay festering. Can you imagine the postures in which Man, once created in the image of his Maker, had been twisted? Do not try, for were you to succeed you would ask yourself, with me: "Can I ever forget?"'[47]

There was another mood. In 1876 Archibald Forbes went to the Balkans to report the fighting between Turkey and Serbia. 'From the point of view of the war correspondent', he wrote later, 'the campaign ... fairly bristled with adventure .... There were few days on which a man ... could not, somehow or other, find a fight in which to enjoy himself.'[48] From South Africa in 1900 Churchill wrote:

> Those who live under the conditions of a civilised city ... gain luxury at the expense of joy . But the soldier ... wakes in an elation of body and spirit without an effort and with scarcely a yawn. There is no more delicious moment in the day than this, when we light the fire ... knowing that there is another whole day begun ... free from all cares. All cares - for who can be worried about the little matters of humdrum life when he may be dead before night? ... Here life itself, life at its best and healthiest, awaits the caprice of a bullet. Let us see the development of the day. All else may stand over, perhaps for ever. Existence is never so sweet as when it is at hazard.[49]

Here fact and fiction meet, for this is exactly what boys' adventure stories say: boys enjoy fighting, men enjoy war. After the battle of Ulundi in July 1879 Bandsman Joseph Banks of the 90th Light Infantry wrote to his wife that he 'was one of the lucky ones and sent with the regiment, being a fighting soldier for a day and not a bandsman.' A non-commissioned officer of the 17th Lancers had a splendid time at the same battle: 'We had a glorious go in, old boy, pig-sticking was a fool to it.' Nearly twenty years later G. E. Steevens, reporting Kitchener's reconquest of the Sudan, went unarmed with the attacking force at the battle of the Atbara and his description of the action is all in a tone of fierce delight. Of Lieutenant-Colonel Forbes of the Warwickshire Regiment he said: 'I saw him enjoying himself like a schoolboy with a half-holiday' and of some wounded privates whom he spoke to after the battle: 'It was not the unhappiest day in these men's lives either.'[50]

For those on the losing side war was less enjoyable, as letters written from Zululand after a British force had been destroyed at Isandhlwana show,[51] and all soldiers in the field have to put up with boredom and with hardship varying from minor inconvenience to starvation. Nevertheless there is such a thing as the joy of battle. Wolseley, describing his experience as a subaltern storming a stockade in Burma in 1853, says: 'you are for the time being ... lifted up from and out of all petty thoughts of self, and for a moment your whole existence, soul and body, seems to revel in a true sense of glory.'[52]

This is a gentleman's view of war, war seen neither as politics nor as a manifestation of the will of God, but simply as the most testing, the most exciting, the most satisfying, the most honourable of field-sports, and field-sports, especially hunting, had for centuries made up a large part, if not the main part, of the lives of the gentlemen of England. Nothing gave a gentleman greater prestige in his county, which was what most of them chiefly cared about, than riding hard to hounds, and proficiency in other sporting activities followed close behind. The word 'gentleman', in origin, has nothing to do with gentleness but a great deal to do with gentility, the bearing of arms, the waging of war. For war hunting is excellent training, requiring an eye for country, decisiveness, stamina and courage.

Officers of all arms and both services were encouraged to hunt: not just cavalry officers but infantrymen, gunners, engineers and naval officers as well. Admiral Beatty (1871-1936), the most popular naval hero of the Great War, hunted all his life and broke his jaw at it after his retirement. Admiral Cradock (1862-1914) wished he might die in action or in the hunting field.[53] He had his first choice on a stormy November afternoon in the South Pacific off Coronel. Behind the lines of Torres Vedras, in the Peninsular War, British officers hunted the fox. In Peshawar Vale, from the mid-nineteenth century until the end of British rule in India, they hunted jackal. Wherever the British army went its officers hunted something. Colonel R. S. S. Baden-Powell (1857-1941), later a lieutenant-general, later still Chief Scout, was emphatic about the military value of pig-sticking: 'the best of all hunts - namely, the pursuit, with a good weapon in your hand, of an enemy whom you want to kill.' 'Pig-sticking', he said, 'is ... *par excellence* a soldier's sport; it tests, develops, and sustains his best service qualities, and stands without rival as a training-school for officers; nor is it ever likely to languish for want of votaries so long as boars and Britons continue to exist.'[54]

B.-P.'s view of sport as a training for war and the related view of war as the best possible kind of sport was widely held. An aristocratic captain of the 60th Rifles, writing to his father from Zululand in 1879, said he was rather ashamed to own it, but he liked the life: 'it is to me like a shooting expedition, with just a spice of danger thrown in to make it really interesting.'[55] An infantry officer writing in 1916 unconsciously echoed this sentiment: 'When war broke out, the public-school man applied for his commission in the firm conviction that war was a glorified form of big-game hunting - the highest form of sport.'[56] Major-General J. F. C. Fuller, in his book on the Boer War, recalled that as a young officer he 'had been brought up to believe that war was a sport, and that the height of soldiership was to be a sportsman.'[57] Another Boer War veteran evidently regretted the invention of firearms:

> it is the manner more than the number of the losses caused by any visitation which causes it to live horribly in the memory for ever. There could have been little of the horrible when men galloped joyously at each other lance in rest, or stoutly faced each other afoot, eyes watching eyes over the bayonet point, every muscle alive to the splendid sport of fighting.[58]

A retired captain of the Leicestershire Regiment, writing for schoolboys just before 1914, referred to 'the great and terribly serious game of war.'[59] So far as views of this kind were founded on personal experience of war, they were founded chiefly on the late nineteenth-century wars of the British Empire. To that majestic institution, that indispensable centrepiece of national self-consciousness and self-confidence, we now turn.

CHAPTER THREE

The British Empire:
'Dominion over palm and pine'

' "The Empire upon which the sun never sets." We all know these words, and we say them with a somewhat proud and grand air, for that vast Empire is ours. It belongs to us, and we to it.' These words, aimed at schoolchildren, open Miss H. E. Marshall's *Our Empire Story,* published in 1908 and reissued time and again until the late 1960's. Miss Marshall was neither the first nor the only author in this field. Dr W. H. Fitchett, Principal of the Methodist Ladies' College, Melbourne, published *Deeds that Won the Empire* in 1897 and *Fights for the Flag* in 1898. Each was a collection of pieces written for the *Melbourne Argus.*

By 1900 *Deeds that Won the Empire,* published in London by Smith, Elder & Co., was in its twelfth edition. 'The tales here told', Dr Fitchett wrote in the Preface, 'are written, not to glorify war, but to nourish patriotism. They represent an effort to renew in popular memory the great traditions of the Imperial race to which we belong.' 'Anything that can help the young mind to appreciate the value and might of the British Empire ... must be for the benefit of posterity', wrote a flamboyant naval hero, Lord Charles Beresford (1846-1919), in 1908, recommending *The Children's Encyclopaedia*.[1] In 1911 Rudyard Kipling (1865-1936) and C. R. L. Fletcher (1857-1934), an opinionated Oxford don, collaborated in *A School History of England.* Kipling's contribution was verse, mostly bad, though a reviewer in the *Daily Express* thought well of it and commented: 'there never was a time so much as the present when the young minds of England are anxious to learn what has gone to the making of the great Empire of which they will grow up to be citizens.'[2]

Books the future soldiers of the Great War might or might not read. Imperial pride they would soak up by a process of total immersion from early childhood onward. They would be swept along on the emotional tides generated by Queen Victoria's jubilees, by the outbreak of the Boer War, by the relief of Mafeking, by the coronations of King Edward VII and King George V. During the Boer War they might wear tin buttons with portraits of Buller, Roberts, Baden-Powell, Kitchener, and they might use pottery similarly adorned. The Singer Sewing Machine Company in 1900 produced bookmarks carrying coloured portraits of the Queen, Roberts and Kitchener. Anyone suspected of being a 'pro-Boer' might have his error forcibly pointed out to him. Jubilees and coronations produced mugs, given by thousands to children, with royal portraits and imperial titles. All coins from 1897 onward carried the abbreviation *Ind. Imp.* and no doubt its meaning, translated as 'Empress [Emperor] of India', was widely known.

In the Empire Music Hall and in many other places patriotic songs were sung. At a higher musical level Edward Elgar's *Coronation Ode* of 1902 contains the tune for which A. C. Benson (1862-1925) provided words beginning 'Land of Hope and Glory', which in a later version included the couplet:

Wider still and wider shall thy bounds be set.
God, Who made thee mighty, make thee mightier yet.

More ominous sentiments also appear in the Ode:

Britain, ask of thyself, and see that thy sons be strong!
Strong to arise and go, see that thy sons be strong.
See that thy sons be strong, strong to arise and go,
If ever the wartrump peal!

'It was an enterprise', says J. M. MacKenzie, writing of the Empire, 'tinged with a sense of moral crusade, aided by periodic war, led by charismatic figures, both alive and dead. In its ancestor worship, its ritual, its emphasis on authority, it linked tribal atavisms with cultural self-satisfaction and technical advance.'[3]

'Periodic war' was played at by small boys with toy soldiers in red coats, and their opponents were apt to be fuzzy-wuzzies from the Sudan, especially after 1898, or assegai-armed Zulus. It was also plentifully illustrated. Lady Butler (1846-1933) painted *The Roll Call* (Crimean War), *The Remnant of an Army* (First Afghan War, 1839-42), *The Defence of Rorke's Drift* (Zulu War, 1879) and many other episodes of nineteenth-century warfare in the cause of the British Empire. Her research for her paintings was painstaking, so that the detail was as accurate as she could make it, but glory or pathos smothers horror and the result is uplifting rather than disturbing. Her paintings were widely reproduced. So were many others at a lower level of artistic competence and conscientiousness. Innumerable coloured prints of imperial battle scenes portrayed, perhaps, the cutting down of mutinous sepoys in the Mutiny in righteous revenge for the horrors of Cawnpore, or played upon rather similar emotions by showing a wounded nurse, apparently in Wolseley's Egyptian campaign of 1882, being tended by a Highlander while his comrades seek the nurse's dastardly assailants. Pictures such as these hung on cottage walls alongside Queen Victoria.

Geography in Victorian schools taught imperial lessons too. As early as 1848 a map of 'The British Dominions', put out by the National Society for promoting the Education of the Poor told users: 'Colonies under the direct administration of the Crown are coloured RED.' 'Dependent and tributary Territories', which included most of Canada (administered by the

Hudson's Bay Company), the greater part of Australia and the whole of India (under the East India Company) were shown in green. In the early 1850's maps intended for prospective emigrants were using the red convention, and it was well established by the 1870's. Mercator's Projection, widely used for class-room maps of the world, made the Empire look even larger than it really was by exaggerating Canada into an immense red splurge dominating the United States on the upper left-hand side and by magnifying Australia, diagonally opposite, though by contrast India was unfairly diminished.

Every year on 24th May - Queen Victoria's birthday - Empire Day would be celebrated. Schoolchildren might assemble in a public park to sing patriotic songs, which in the 1970's one survivor remembered enjoying. In 1909 the newly-invented and rapidly multiplying Boy Scouts were told by the King that 'the habits of discipline which they are now acquiring as boys will enable them to do their duty as men should any danger threaten the Empire.'[4] From top to bottom of society the Empire enveloped the fabric of society. Even those who belonged to the eccentric minority who disapproved of it could not escape its all-pervading presence.

For most people in Great Britain in 1914, to a degree incomprehensible in the 1980's, the Empire was an indispensable element in their confidence in their nation and in themselves. About 13.1 million square miles and 435 million people (60 million of them white, 315 million in India), or about a quarter of the land area of the world and about a quarter of its inhabitants, were under some form of British authority, direct or indirect. The Canadians could easily justify the claim made on one of their postage stamps, issued at Christmas 1897: 'We hold a vaster Empire than has been.'

Before 1914 Canada, South Africa, Australia and New Zealand were collectively referred to, by their own people as well as by people at home, as 'the colonies'. There were also colonies of black men kept in order by white rulers, but they did not spring so readily to mind. Imperial pride, as the Canadian stamp and Fitchett's writings suggest, flourished as strongly abroad as at home, and when the British throughout the world thought of the Empire they were apt to think first of the four countries which, taken together with Great Britain, Kipling called 'The Five Nations'.

Between the mother country and the colonies personal ties were manifold and close, because in the early twentieth century the tide of emigration from Great Britain had for many years been running strongly. In the last fifty years of the nineteenth century between eight million and nine million people (over three million of them Irish) left the United Kingdom. In the years 1911-13 the outward flood was at its peak. Nearly 1.4 million people left, several hundreds of them in the *Titanic*.[5] This outward-flowing human tide, as late as 1937, was called to mind in the Canadian National Railways' trains by three classes of passenger accomodation: Standard (first), Tourist (second) and Colonist (third). Colonists' seating was upholstered, but although they might spend several days in a train they were not provided with sleeping berths.

Many emigrants, including probably most of the Irish, went to the USA and some emigrants came back. Nevertheless by the time war broke out a large proportion of the 15 million or so white people in 'the colonies' must have been first- or second-generation immigrants with recent and on the whole affectionate memories of 'the old country' and close family ties there, kept up or not as the case might be. The strength of colonial attachment was demonstrated by the numbers who volunteered for service in the Sudan in 1885, for the Boer War about fifteen years later, and for the Great War. 'Colonials' looked upon theselves as British - or, as most would probably have said, English - as well as being Canadians, South Africans, Australians or New Zealanders.

People at home were often patronising about 'colonials'. They were apt to regard them as uncouth and they might hold, according to a New Zealander writing in 1906, 'the ludicrous idea that the Englishman who stays at home is superior to the Englishman who doesn't.'[6] A more flattering view emerges from this description of a mounted patrol during the Boer War:

> Out they go, fifty picturesque brown horsemen, with shaggy nags and 'smasher' hats and a general leathery cowboy look. What is it about our irregular horse that makes a lump rise in the throat as one sees them streaming along at a canter, big, fit, sunburnt men, with an air about them that makes one think also of the boundlessness of an Empire which pours such men from its almost unknown recesses?[7]

This was the conventional picture of 'colonials' - 'picturesque brown horsemen ... leathery ... big, fit, sunburnt.' Town-dwelling Australians and Canadians may not have been noticeably better horsemen or more leathery than Londoners, but it was good for colonials' self-esteem to think of themselves as hardy frontiersmen and it was encouraging for those at home to see them as such. It did something to set off the fear expressed by Lieutenant-General Sir Robert Baden-Powell in 1907 that 'the same causes which brought about the downfall of the Great Roman Empire were working to-day in Great Britain.'[8]

The foundation and growth of the colonies seemed to demonstrate almost any desirable national chracteristic that anyone cared to name - commercial enterprise, seamanship, puritan morals, political genius (after suitable lessons had been learnt from the American Revolution). In Tennyson's words:

'We sailed wherever ship could sail,
We founded many a mighty state',

and there was the comforting thought expressed in the Report of the 1851 Census: 'the people of the new nations maintain an indissoluble union with the parent country.'[9]

If for most people the colonies came first to mind when the Empire was mentioned, then close second came India, not in any sense a 'colony' but equally gratifying to British self-esteem. The conquest of India demonstrated what Winston Churchill in 1897 called 'the firm step of an Imperial people.' The 'Imperial people' marvelled at their own ability to govern a population of over 300 million through fewer than 2,000 British officials supported by about 75,000 British troops. 'I was arrogant enough', said a private soldier of a later generation, speaking on BBC television of his service in India, 'to believe that the English were very good at governing other people.'[10] So were the Victorians, with good reason.

By comparison with the colonies and India the rest of the Empire made little impression. Children's writers scarcely nodded towards it, sometimes not even that. H. E. Marshall made no attempt to deal with any British possessions except the major ones, merely remarking in her preface: 'perhaps, some day ... I will tell you in another book more stories of Our Empire.' C. R. L. Fletcher spoke of 'the vast territory of Rhodesia, in the centre of the dark continent of Africa, and ... Uganda, British East Africa and British Central Africa farther to the North ... still, as yet, more or less undeveloped.' He dismissed them in ten lines ending: 'The natives everywhere welcome the justice and mercy of our rule, and they are no longer liable to be carried off as slaves by Arab slave-dealers.' The West African colonies he did not mention and the West Indies he dismissed magisterially: 'In such a climate a few bananas will sustain the life of a negro quite sufficently; why should he work to get more than this? He is quite happy and quite useless, and spends any extra wages which he may earn upon finery.' Ward Lock's *Wonder Book of Empire,* first issued just before the Great War and many times re-issued later, as bland as Fletcher is biting, made some attempt to be comprehensive, but although the West Indies were listed among British possessions they were not discussed.[11]

By 1914 patriotism and imperialism were interdependent. For most Englishmen the one was hardly credible without the other, whether they approved of the two sentiments or not - even, perhaps, if they sympathised with the workman who is reported as saying, in 1906, 'All I want is victuals.

What's the British Empire? Damn the British Empire!' Yet imperialism in its modern sense was scarcely more than a generation old. During the first half of Queen Victoria's reign the word was associated more readily with despotic continental empires, including the Holy Roman Empire, than with the dominions of Queen Victoria.

The early Victorians directed their abundant political energies chiefly towards free trade and parliamentary reform. Their ideals lay rather in the direction of universal peace than of universal dominion. The Great Exhibition of 1851 was their exuberant assertion of British commercial and industrial supremacy, not a display of imperial power. The exhibitors' medal carries the emollient inscription, taken from Ovid, *Metamorphoses* I 25, DISSOCIATA LOCIS CONCORDI PACE LIGAVIT - roughly: 'He has bound together in peace things from widely separated places': hardly the equivalent in sentiment of 'Wider still and wider shall thy bounds be set.' Orthodox opinion at mid-century was inclined to regard them 'as a sort of encumbered estate the cost of whose maintenance outweighed the dignity of its possession.'[12]

Nevertheless by the early 1850's, with a steadily rising flow of emigrants towards the colonies, there were signs of change in sentiment. The convention of colouring British possessions red on the map (p. 37 above) was being established, and in 1852 Letts, Son & Steer, the publishers of H. Smith Evans's 'A Map and Guide to all the Emigration Colonies of Great Britain and America', decorated it with the most famous of all short statements of British national pride: 'Britain upon whose Empire the Sun never Sets.'

II

'To persons whose memory reaches back beyond the days of the Crimean War,' wrote Edward Dicey, aged 66, in 1898, 'there are few things more striking ... than the change in popular sentiment with respect to our colonial empire.'[13]. Along with that change, and moving in the same direction, went a change in sentiment towards the army, brought about by events in the Crimea. Traditional fears that a standing army might be used to support an oppressive government, though not extinct (the deployment of troops during the Chartist unrest of the early 1840's was very recent) were less acute, perhaps, when war broke out than in times gone by. Then the bravery of the troops, their sufferings before Sebastopol in the winter of 1854-5, and Florence Nightingale's achievements at Scutari, all reported as war had never been reported before, transformed the British Army's public relations. The suspicion which had hung over the army from Cromwell's time until Wellington's faded away. It became possible, and journalists, poets, artists and publicists of all kinds seized the possibility, to present the soldier not as a brutal ne'er-do-well hired to threaten the liberties of honest Englishmen (Irishmen were another matter) but as a noble fellow.

Rough, untutored, even drunken the soldier might be, but of his manly virtues there could be no doubt. In the 1860's the Professor of Poetry at Oxford, Sir Francis Doyle (1810-88) went to the heart of the matter. He took as his subject Private Moyse who, captured by the Chinese, and 'declaring that he would not prostrate himself before any Chinaman alive, was immediately knocked upon the head, and his body thrown on a dunghill:'

> Last night, among his fellow roughs,
> He jested, quaffed, and swore;
> A drunken private of the Buffs,
> Who never looked before.
>
> To-day, beneath the foeman's frown,
> He stands in Elgin's place,
> Ambassador from Britain's crown
> And type of all her race.[14]

When the Crimean War ended in April 1856, the army's popularity already stood high.[15] In May 1857 the Indian Mutiny broke out and carried it higher. No war, perhaps, could have been better calculated to do so. India was for most people in Great Britain a strange, distant land full of palm trees, poisonous snakes and the heathen, of small direct interest except to the few who might hope to find employment in the East India Company's service, to Lancashire cotton manufacturers, and to missionaries. It was often the scene of bloody and occasionally disastrous warfare, in which British victory could by no means be taken for granted. It was not, in 1857, the glittering symbol of national greatness which it later became. Nevertheless the Mutiny was an intolerable insult to British authority. Moreover the mutinous sepoys perpetrated horrible outrages and perpetrated some of them, what was more, against British women and children. The British were heavily and romantically outnumbered. Some of the generals were known to be practising Christians of the most approved puritanical kind. Heroic deeds were rewarded with a new emblem, instituted in 1856, which, unlike any other decoration, was for officers and men alike. It was the Victoria Cross.

Here were all the ingredients for a powerful brew of military hero-worship and imperial pride. They were stirred together in plentiful literature which for half a century and more the Mutiny generated. A crop of great names - Henry Lawrence (1806-57), killed defending Lucknow; his brother John (1811-79) 'the saviour of the Punjab'; John Nicholson (1821-57) 'the Hero of Delhi'; James Outram (1803-63) 'the Bayard of India'; William Hodson (1821-58) who raised Hodson's Horse and shot two Mogul princes who attempted to rescue the King of Delhi; Colin Campbell, Lord Clyde (1792-1863), who became the main architect of victory; Henry Havelock (1795-1857), the austere puritan who recaptured Cawnpore - provided a rich harvest for biographers at all levels, from Bosworth Smith's two volumes on John Lawrence to F. W. Holmes's *Four Heroes of India* (Clive, Warren Hastings, Henry Havelock, John Lawrence), aimed at the Sunday School prize market.

Captain L J Trotter specialised in Indian biography. Forty years after the Mutiny his *Life of John Nicholson* went into six editions within a year of publication. 'His [Nicholson's] heroic figure', wrote Trotter, 'has marched across many a page of commemorative print', and when Trotter's *The Bayard of India,* first published in 1903, appeared in 1909 - over fifty years after the Mutiny - in J. M. Dent's Everyman's Library Ernest Rhys remarked in an introductory note: 'the rapid evolution of new democratic ideas ... has given a keener reflected interest to [Britain's] military annals.' The observation has a fine ironic edge to it in an age which has dispensed with heroes. The men of the Mutiny, even the greatest of them, even the Lawrences, are forgotten, so thoroughly has imperial glory been expunged from the public consciousness.

In heavyweight history, Sir John Kaye (1814-76) wrote a three-volume *History of the Sepoy War,* revised and continued up to six volumes by Colonel G. B. Malleson (1825-98). W. H. Russell's *My Diary in India,* published in 1859 and many times reprinted, is distinguished by frequent frank comments on atrocities committed by the British - 'spiritual and mental tortures to which we have no right to resort, and which we dare not perpetrate in the face of Europe.'[16] Interest in the Mutiny was still strong enough in the 1890's to encourage Lady Inglis to publish *The Siege of Lucknow* in 1891 and William Forbes-Mitchell his *Reminiscences of the Great Mutiny* in 1893. Lady Inglis was the widow of a major-general who, as a brigadier, succeeded to the command at Lucknow after Sir Henry Lawrence was killed. Forbes-Mitchell was a sergeant in the 93rd Highlanders. He commented bitterly on the quality of British sword-blades compared with native weapons. Lady Inglis's book went into at least two editions, Forbes-Mitchell's into at least three printings. Apart from these works dealing solely with the Mutiny, Lord Roberts, Lord Wolseley, Sir Evelyn Wood and other generals told their Mutiny stories in their autobiographies, and for generals' autobiographies there was a strong demand (p. 51 below) at the end of the century and in the early 1900's.

In fiction Flora Annie Steel (1847-1929), deservedly successful in her day but later almost unknown, published *On the Face of the Waters* in 1896 and *Voices in the Night* in 1900. *On the Face of the Waters* is a study of the Mutiny, partly from the mutineers' side. *Voices in the Night,* set in 'Nushapore' - Lucknow thinly disguised - is heavy with Mutiny memories. Mrs Steel was for some time an inspectress of schools in the Punjab. She knew native Indian life, especially Indian women's life, well, and she had a strong sympathy with the Muslim families who had ruled the country under the Moguls and who had lost their employment under the British. Her novels are at least as powerful as Kipling's Indian stories. Henry Newbolt, that indefatigable poet of Empire, was inspired by the Mutiny to write 'A Ballad of John Nicholson'. It begins:

> John Nicholson to Jullundur came
> On his way to Delhi fight

and is best left there, though in its day it was well thought of.

Memorials to the Mutiny are not all literary. In London there are statues of Lord Clyde, Sir Henry Havelock, Lord Lawrence (John Lawrence) and Sir James Outram. No other war, including the Great War, is so plentifully commemorated by monuments to its leading figures.[17] The impact of the Mutiny on the Victorian mind was powerful and lasting: lasting enough to be lively still in the years immediately before 1914. By then it had become one of the legends of Empire.

And yet the nation, at the time of the Mutiny, was not 'imperialist' in outlook. The reported cruelties of the sepoys stirred the nation to fury and stimulated a demand for vengeance without overmuch regard for justice. W. H. Russell's condemnation of British ferocity had less effect on public opinion than his exposure of maladministration during the Crimean War. The Mutiny evoked a fierce determination to assert the British right - the right of conquest - to rule India. It reinforced national pride in the British achievement there and confirmed British belief in British superiority over all other races, especially coloured races. But the war was defensive, fought on the principle 'what we have we hold', not in order to set the bounds of Empire 'wider yet'.

Blood shed in the Mutiny nevertheless watered a soil in which imperial pride could grow, and grow it did, fostered also during the 1860's by disturbing changes in the balance of power in Europe. In 1868 Sir Charles Dilke (1843-1911), at the outset of his career, published a two-volume 'Record of Travel in English-speaking countries during 1866 and 1867' for which he invented the title *Greater Britain*. 'If two small islands', he wrote, 'are by courtesy styled "Great", America, Australia, India must form a Greater Britain', and in discussing the extent of British possessions he gave expression both to a new view of Great Britain's position in the world and to the rising threat of competition, military and industrial, from other powers:

> Their [British possessions'] surface is five times as great as that of the empire of Darius, and $4\frac{1}{2}$ times as large as the Roman Empire at its greatest extent. It is no exaggeration to say that in power the English countries would be more than a match for the remaining nations of the world.

Notwithstanding this robust assertion of confidence, he also remarked uneasily: '... we are forced to contemplate the speedy loss of our manufacturing supremacy as coal becomes cheaper in America and dearer in Old England.'[18]

Dilke was a radical and, in theory, a republican. Disraeli was a Conservative royalist. After he came to power in 1874 the new imperial tone in the national voice was heard repeatedly. In a series of theatrical gestures, mostly towards India, the Prime Minister asserted his country's standing as at least the equal of the continental military empires. By the time he left office in 1880 Her Majesty's Government had become the largest shareholder in the Suez Canal Company in 1875; the Queen, greatly to her own satisfaction, had been proclaimed Empress of India in 1876; Indian troops had been summoned to Malta to impress the Russians in 1878; and a 'forward policy' on the Indian frontier had brought war with Afghanistan in 1879. Besides all that, in 1879 the Zulus were forced into war for the purpose of destroying their impressive military power, but that was not Disraeli's doing. He was not interested in Africa.

On the other side of British politics Gladstone and orthodox Liberals loathed war and imperial aggrandisement. 'Remember the rights of the savage, as we call him', said Gladstone, orating in Midlothian in 1879. 'Remember that the happiness of his humble home, remember that the sanctity of life in the hill villages of Afghanistan, among the winter snows, is as inviolable in the eye of Almighty God as can be your own.'[19] 'False phantoms of glory' were financially and morally abominable (finance and morality were often associated in the Liberal mind): unworthy of the British people and the British Government.

Such notions, though never entirely obliterated, were going out of fashion in the 1870's. On the Stock Exchange, a reliable guide to middle-class opinion, 'a lively demonstration' supported hostility to Russia in 1878, even at the risk of war, even with Consols down to $93\frac{5}{8}$. The crisis produced one of the most famous of all music-hall choruses:

We don't want to fight,
But, by Jingo, if we do,
We've got the ships, we've got the men,
We've got the money too.

To which, when Disraeli sent for Indian troops, a sceptical poet responded:

We don't want to fight,
And, by Jingo, if we do,
We will not go to war ourselves -
We'll send the mild Hindoo.

'Free trade and international exhibitions', wrote T. H. S. Escott (d. 1924), successor to John Morley (1838-1923) as editor of *The Fortnightly Review,* 'have not brought the millenium appreciably nearer to mankind. The military spirit was never stronger in England than to-day , the question, What must England do to retain her traditional place in the nations of the world? never more anxiously discussed.' In 1881 Lord Rosebery, a future Liberal Prime Minister, showed how strongly Liberal opinion was moving against Gladstone and his followers by offering a new definition of 'imperialism': 'I mean the greater pride in Empire which is called Imperialism, a larger patriotism.'[20]

The leading propagandist of this 'larger patriotism', in academic circles, was J. R. Seeley (1834-95), who in 1869 succeeded Charles Kingsley as Professor of Modern History at Cambridge. In 1883 he turned a series of lectures into a short and lively book: *The Expansion of England.* Its success was immediate and lasting. Between 1883 and 1911 it went through two editions and sixteen reprintings and it was still being used at Cambridge in 1914.

Seeley regarded the study of history from a practical point of view, as a guide to political action. No Marxist could have been more explicit. 'We do not now read it for pleasure,' he told his students, 'but in order that we may discover the laws of political growth and change.'[21] He seems to have been strongly influenced by Sir Charles Dilke (p. 44 above), for he considered it absurd to think of English history as most historians thought of it: that is, as the history of England. It ought to be seen as the history of the expansion of England into 'Greater Britain', Dilke's phrase used without acknowledgement to Sir Charles. 'We seem', said Seeley, 'to have conquered and peopled half the world in a fit of absence of mind.'[22]

When he wrote of the British Empire he meant chiefly 'four great groups of territory, inhabited either chiefly or to a large extent by Englishmen and subject to the Crown, and a fifth great territory subject to the Crown and ruled by English officials, but inhabited by a completely foreign race.' He meant, that is to say, 'the colonies' and India. 'Colonies', he said, 'are neither more nor less than a great augmentation of the national estate. They are lands for the landless, prosperity and wealth for those in straitened circumstances.' In them lay the chief hope for the nation's future.[23]

Prosperous colonies might fall away into independence and the fashionable mid-century view, coloured by fairly recent experience in America, had been that they would and, if they would, let them. No more wars of independence! To Seeley this was wrong-headed. It was the old colonial system that had driven the Americans to rebel, and in rebelling they had destroyed the old colonial system. Seeley was in no doubt about what should take its place:

> If the colonies are not ... possessions of England, then they must be a part of England ... We must cease altogether to say that England is an island off the north-western coast of Europe, that it has an area of 120,000 square miles and a population of thirty odd millions. We must cease to think that emigrants, when they go to the colonies, leave England or are lost to England ... When we have accustomed ourselves to contemplate the whole Empire together and call it all England, we shall see that here too is a United States. Here too is a great homogeneous people, one in blood, language, religion and laws, but dispersed over a boundless space. [24]

This view of Empire, as Dilke had found, was immensely encouraging. It promised lasting power and greatness for England in a world increasingly dominated by large states; power and greatness, moreover, which no other European nation could hope to rival, for no other European nation had its own people so widely scattered over the globe. 'If the United States and Russia hold together for another half-century', said Seeley with remarkable foresight, 'they will ... completely dwarf France and Germany and depress them into a second class. They will do the same to England, if at the end of that time England still thinks of herself as simply a European State, as the old United Kingdom of Great Britain and Ireland, such as Pitt left her.' If, on the other hand, the Empire, apart from India, were to be looked on as 'a vast English nation', no such eclipse was likely.

> Greater Britain ... will belong to the stronger class of political unions. If it will not be stronger than the United States, we may say with confidence that it will be far stronger than the great conglomeration of Slavs, Germans, Turcomans and Armenians, of Greek Christians, Catholics, Protestants, Mussulmans and Buddhists, which we call Russia.[25]

British rule in India Seeley regarded with mixed astonishment and practicality. 'Nothing great that has ever been done by Englishmen', he said, 'was done so unintentionally, so accidentally, as the conquest of India', but he doubted whether the material advantages which it brought, chiefly in trade, were worth the burden it imposed: 'India, at the same time as it locks up an army, more than doubles the difficulty of our foreign policy.' Yet 'our Government is better than any other which has existed in India since the Mussulman conquest' and to leave the country would be 'the most inexcusable of all crimes, and might possibly cause the most stupendous of all conceivable calamities.' Of the latent power of Indian nationalism he had no illusions: 'if there could arise in India a nationality movement ... the English power must succumb at once.' His forecasts were lamentably accurate, but he hardly seems to have believed in them. 'The abandonment of India is an idea which even those who believe that we shall some day be driven to it are not accustomed to contemplate as a practical scheme', and in the meantime the existence of the Indian Empire convinced him of the racial superiority of his compatriots: 'There need be no question about the general fact that the ruling race in British India has a higher and more vigorous civilisation than the native races.'[26]

Seeley, exceptionally lucky or exceptionally shrewd - perhaps both - published *The Expansion of England* just at the right moment to have the greatest possible impact on practical politics. His view of 'the colonies' as Greater Britain matched the tone of imperialist thought in the years to come; so did his picture of the British Empire as one of the great world states of the twentieth century. Rational in tone and addressed to an academic audience, Seeley's book must have helped to make imperialism respectable in influential circles by containing its rising head of emotional steam within an apparently solid framework of reason. 'Learn to think Imperially', said Joseph Chamberlain (1836-1914) in 1904, and again: 'the day of small nations has long passed away, the day of Empires has come.'[27] The greatest demagogue of the day, speaking first in London and then in Birmingham, was handing on ideas addressed by Dilke and Seeley, in print, to a more restricted audience.

III

Seeley's book was published in the 1880's, a decade full of imperial splendours and miseries. In 1881 647 British soldiers, unwisely posted on Majuba Hill in Natal during a quarrel with the Boers, were chased off it with the loss of 223 killed and wounded. Gladstone, to the fury of imperialists at home, made peace without taking vengeance. 'This ghastly attempt', as Fr Ryder (p. 23 above) called it, 'to foist a Sunday school conscience behind the iron ribs of war'[28] was long remembered against Gladstone. In 1882, in quelling a rising of Egyptians against the Khedive, a

British fleet bombarded Alexandria and Wolseley won the battle of Tel-el-Kebir which led to the British occupation of Egypt and all its consequences down to the fiasco on the Suez Canal in 1956. At the Berlin Conference of 1884, fifteen powers acknowledged the 'scramble for Africa'. The rules of the empire-building game, a very rough one, were laid down not only for Africa but for the world as a whole. In Asia, a British protectorate was set up in North Borneo in 1885 and in 1886 Burma became part of the Indian Empire.

Of the imperial events of the 1880's, two above the rest caught the public imagination and stirred public emotion: the death of General Gordon at Khartoum in 1885 and the Queen's Golden Jubilee in 1887. To these might be added, in a different category, the response to Gladstone's attempt to grant home rule to Ireland in 1886. It demonstrated the intense indignation generated by any hint of a move towards breaking up the Empire.

The spectacle of Gordon at Khartoum, facing savage hordes alone, and of his death in romantic circumstances (stage-managed by himself) with the advance party of Wolseley's relief expedition only a couple of days' journey away, had a dramatic quality unparalleled since the Indian Mutiny. It produced a comparable outburst of emotion at home. This time, moreover, there was a villain at home - Gladstone. National wrath could be directed at him as well as at the distant Mahdi.

Gordon was instructed, acting on the authority of the Khedive, to withdraw Egyptian troops from the Sudan and abandon it to the Mahdi. This he understood perfectly well, but when he arrived in Khartoum he made no attempt to carry his instructions out. Instead, relying on feeling at home against the policy of withdrawal, he blackmailed the British Government into sending British troops into the Sudan. There was accordingly a great deal to be said on Gladstone's behalf and against Gordon but that was not what the nation wanted to know. Reason was nothing, emotion was all. 'The picture of a wonderful life', wrote Sir William Butler (1838-1910), another eminent and unconventional soldier, 'had to be made perfect by heroic death.'[29] The figure of the romantic hero half in love with death, especially death in the Empire's cause, is one we have already met in Admiral Cradock (p. 33 above) and one we shall meet again on our way to the Great War.

Before he went to Khartoum Major-General C G 'Chinese' Gordon (1833-85), an officer of the Royal Engineers, was chiefly known, if known at all, for extraordinary exploits in command of Chinese troops suppressing the Taiping rebellion of the 1860's. As soon as he was ordered to Khartoum, the powerful Victorian machine of mass communication, fuelled with material from his astonishing career in China and elsewhere, built him rapidly into a popular hero of a kind nowadays not only extinct but unimaginable. He was a general, and generals in Victorian and Edwardian times could attract the same kind of adulation as footballers attract in the 1980's. He asserted British authority over races as diverse as the Chinese and the Arabs, and he asserted it by force of character rather than by material power, for his most famous adventures did not take place on British territory or at the head of British troops but as an officer of the Emperor of China or the Khedive of Egypt, and in their dominions. He was admired for devout puritanical Christianity and for charitable exertions on behalf of the poor, especially boys from ragged schools, many of whom he took into his house and started in life by sending them to sea. He never married and women seem to have had little attraction for him. Perhaps he was homosexual, but the unspeakable was never spoken and his work among boys was praised.

Gordon's character, as publicly exhibited, agreed very well with the standard specification for a hero of his day. Most of the qualities attributed to him - bravery in the field, power over savages, puritanism - can be found in other heroes of fact and fiction. Celibacy or late marriage, with obvious advantages for empire-builders in remote and perilous outposts, was also approved of, and the principal women in heroes' lives, as for instance in Baden-Powell's until late middle age, were often their mothers. In fiction, many of Kipling's characters and, later, John Buchan's, are unmarried, as is Sherlock Holmes - though not Dr Watson. Among imperial figures of the first rank, Lord Kitchener (1850-1916) and Cecil Rhodes (1853-1902) never married. Lord Lugard (1858-1925) married at 42; Lord Baden-Powell at 55; Lord Milner (1854-1925) when he was nearly 70.

Gordon's self-justifying *Journal at Khartoum* was published within a few months of his death and at least one *Life* appeared before the end of 1885, the year in which he died. More followed, including Sir William Butler's, already quoted. It was published in 1889 and by 1904 it had been reprinted ten times. Two biographies of Gordon appeared under very similar sub-titles: *'The Christian Soldier and Hero'* and *'A Christian Hero'*, this last written by Lieutenant-Colonel Seton Churchill whose other works include *Lay Work in the Army, Stepping-stones to Higher Things* and *Forbidden Fruit for Young Men*. Biographies of Gordon were excellent material for school prizes, and the two aggressively Christian ones may have been aimed at Sunday schools. *'The Christian Soldier and Hero'* was given as a prize at a Sunday school in Weston-super-Mare in 1917, over thirty years after Gordon's death. As late as 1966 a major film was made about him: a quite exceptional honour, at that period, for an imperial hero. God, Empire and Charles Gordon made a potent trinity.

The later wars of Queen Victoria's Empire produced a plentiful crop of hero-generals, two of the principal ones being Lord Wolseley (1833-1913) and his rival Lord Roberts (1832-1914). Wolseley never quite retrieved his reputation after he failed to rescue Gordon in 1885. Roberts, nearing the age of 70, made himself a super-hero when he cancelled the early disasters of the Boer War by capturing Pretoria. He had a reputation for great popularity with the troops. It endeared him to the growing mass of newspaper-readers and gave him an advantage over Wolseley who 'never won their affection ... nor did he want it.'[30]

In 1897, before his South African apotheosis, Roberts scored 'the greatest success of the last few publishing seasons'[31] with his two-volume autobiography *Forty-One Years in India,* which went into at least five editions in the year in which it first appeared. There was a lively market in field-marshals' memoirs, usually, like Roberts's, in two volumes. Wolseley's *Story of a Soldier's Life* came out in 1903 and in 1906 Sir Evelyn Wood (1838-1919) published *From Midshipman to Field-Marshal* (Wood had the unusual distinction, for a field-marshal, of having started his career in the Royal Navy). The book went through four editions in two volumes in the year of publication and went into a fifth edition, in one volume, the year after: quite why there was so great a demand is difficult, in the 1980's, to discern. Major-General Sir George Younghusband (1859-1944) of the Indian Army published *A Soldier's Memories* in 1917. It was not to be expected that these officers would present a view of war that was either depressing or forbidding, especially since none, since the Crimea, had been called upon to serve in a major war between great European powers, and there had been no general war in Europe since Waterloo.

Successful commanders, like successful sportsmen at a later date, were rewarded with honours from the Crown, which in the commanders' case could run as high as earldoms. Material rewards were very substantial too, again like the rewards of sportsmen two or three generations later, except that the generals' rewards usually came as parliamentary grants. Horatio Bottomley (1860-1933), one of the more flamboyant characters of pre-1914 journalism, did not share the prevailing uncritical adulation of fashionable generals. He recalled in *John Bull* the grant to Lord Roberts after the Boer War, and compared it with the treatment of the rank and file. 'We are unable to forget the enormous, nay, the wicked sum of money [£100,000] ... voted to his Lordship when he represented that he had won the Boer War.' Of Sir John French (1852-1925) Bottomley remarked in 1908: 'there are those who shake their heads at the thought of French taking the supreme command in a great war.'[32] Sir John, in 1914, became commander-in-chief of the British Expeditionary Force in France. Bottomley was unpopular with the Establishment, and no wonder.

The cult of the general as hero was at its height in the early months of the Great War. In September 1914 it found its symbol in Alfred Leete's figure of Kitchener beckoning recruits. Leete created a figure commanding, threatening, shaming; a figure as compelling now as then; a figure which people snigger at as they often snigger at anything which stirs feelings deeper and more disturbing than they care to admit. The fame of Herbert Horatio, Earl Kitchener of Khartoum and of Broome (1850-1916), rested on his reconquest of the Sudan in 1898, just over thirteen years after the death of Gordon, which it was seen to avenge. The war was justified. The benefits of British rule, exercised in a 'condominium' with Egypt, were similar on a smaller scale to the benefits following from British victories in India in the early nineteenth century. In both cases settled rule replaced bloodstained anarchy. With that, however, we are less concerned than with the national mood of heady exaltation which was in the background of the Sudan victory.

The Sudan war, unlike the Indian wars, was fought during the most exuberant, least rational phase of Victorian imperialism. The emotions which it aroused were correspondingly extravagant. Other manifestations of the same public mood were the reaction to Dr Jameson's raid into the Transvaal in 1896 and the furore over Major Marchand's arrival at Fashoda in 1898, which came fairly close to setting off war with France. The patriotic furnace at home was assiduously stoked by the war correspondents at the front. They could communicate rapidly with a large readership, much of it ill-educated.

The tone of public feeling can be caught from two rising young men of very different background but similar outlook: *The Morning Post's* 23-year-old special correspondent Winston Churchill and G W Steevens, at 28 on the staff of the two-year-old *Daily Mail*. The intensity of enthusiasm at home may be gauged from the fact that Steevens's book *With Kitchener to Khartum,* published at the end of September 1898, within a month of the battle of Omdurman, was in its eleventh edition before the end of the year.

Churchill's general view of war (p. 32 above) was equivocal. On the one hand it was 'a dirty, shoddy business'. On the other, it was a glorious adventure and not usually, in imperial campaigns, intolerably dangerous. Discussing 'the odd and bizarre potentates [including Kitchener's opponent, the Khalifa] against whom British arms continually are turned', he remarks:

> Perhaps the time will come when ... there will be no more royal freaks to conquer. In that gloomy period there will be no more of these nice little

expeditions - "the image of European war without its guilt and only twenty-five per cent of its danger"; no more medals for the soldiers, no more peerages for the generals, no more copy for the journalists. The good old times will have passed away, and ... though the world may not be much more prosperous it can scarcely be so merry.

Merry, no doubt, for the imperial forces, armed with what Churchill describes elswhere as 'the powerful weapons of civilisation - the shrapnel shell, the magazine rifle, and the Maxim gun' - that is, the weapons of the Great War. What of their opponents, the 'savages who had for many years afflicted the Sudan and cumbered the earth'? At Omdurman, against a total loss to Kitchener's forces of about 500 killed and wounded, or 2 per cent, the Dervish losses have been put at 15,000 or 30 per cent, though no accuracy is possible.

In other imperial battles also the proportionate losses were unequal. At the Atbara river, during Kitchener's approach march in 1898, the British losses were 4 per cent (570 of 14,000) against estimated Dervish losses of 5,000 out of 18,000 (28 per cent). In 1895 in India, at the Malakand Pass, the British lost 0.5 per cent of 15,000 (75) against their enemies' 500 or so of 12,000 (4 per cent). At Tel-el-Kebir in 1882, Wolseley's army of 17,000 lost 339 men - 2 per cent - against 'very heavy' Egyptian losses. Figures can be quoted the other way - British losses at Isandhlwana, for instance, in 1879, or at Maiwand in 1880 were almost certainly much heavier than losses on the other side - but in most imperial wars the British casualty figures were not high enough to damp the enthusiasm with which they were fought.[33]

Steevens, much more than Churchill, was in love with violence for its own sake. He calls Kitchener, whom he greatly admired, 'the man who has cut out his human heart and made himself a machine to retake Khartum.' Battles are described with enthusiastic ferocity. He revels in the scene of the entry of the army into Berber after the battle of the Atbara. Kitchener, at the head of his men, 'passed under a triumphal arch, and all the street was Venetian masts and bunting and coloured paper ... and men and women and children shrieking shrill delight.' In a clear space between the columns came the captured Dervish commander Mahmud, his hands tied behind his back. It is said, though not by Steevens, that he was driven on with whips. 'It was more like a Roman triumph than anything you have ever seen' - in that age of classical education the resemblance is unlikely to have been accidental - 'like in its colour, its barbarism, its intoxicating arrogance.' All very stirring, no doubt, for readers of The Daily Mail. 'You may call the show barbaric, if you like. It was meant for barbarians. The English gentleman, if you like, is half barbarian, too. That is just the value of him.' Later in his book Steevens returns to the same theme. Writing of the Sudan he says: 'Perhaps to Englishmen - half savage still on the pinnacle of their civilisation - the very charm of the land lies still in its empty barbarism ... You are left a savage again - a savage with Rosbach water, if there is any left, and a Mauser repeating pistol-carbine, if the sand has not jammed it, but still at the last word a savage. You are a naked man, facing naked nature.'[34]

These sentiments were not unique to Steevens. They were widespread, though not often so articulately expressed. Two soldiers, H. S. L. Alford and the aptly named W. D. Sword, also hurried into print in 1898. They were equally explicit:

> Full information of the doings of our soldiers and sailors encourages a strong national and patriotic feeling, binding the nation closer in a common enthusiasm ... The love of victory and conquest is still strong within us, and the lust for war by the great nations of the world at the present time is only curbed by the fear of ... defeat.

Before the victorious British in the Sudan a brilliant prospect opened:

> The recapture of the Soudan will ... bring into possibility the great Imperial aspiration of opening up the vast area of Central Africa. A British railway running from Cairo to the Cape will be an achievement of the near future: a colony under the British flag, stretching from end to end of the African continent is ... within the range of practical politics, and Great Britain will allow nothing to stand in the way.[35]

This conception of war in an imperial cause as glorious in itself and profitable in its results could readily soar away from its roots in hard practicality and flower into irrational romanticism strongly tinged with a death wish. The crippled poet W. E. Henley (1849-1903), who greatly admired G. W. Steevens, had caught the mood as early as 1891 when he published a highly successful anthology, *Lyra Heroica,* which was still being reprinted in 1921. In his Preface he wrote:

> This book of verse for boys is, I believe, the first of its kind in England ... To set forth, as only art can, the beauty and the joy of living, the beauty and the blessedness of death, the glory of battle and adventure, the nobility of devotion - to a cause, an ideal, a passion even - the dignity of resistance, the sacred quality of patriotism, that is my ambition here.

Henley's poem 'The Song of the Sword', dedicated to Rudyard Kipling, includes the lines:

> Arch-anarch, chief builder, Prince and evangelist,
> I am the Will of God:
> I am the Sword.[36]

Nor was this mood dissipated, as is sometimes suggested, by the shocks of reality in the Boer War. Christopher Stone (1882-1965), who was appointed to the Distinguished Service Order and awarded a Military Cross in the Great War and went on to become one of the cosier figures of the BBC under Lord Reith, published in 1908 an anthology called *War Songs*. General Sir Ian Hamilton (1853-1947) wrote an introduction.

General Hamilton had seen a great deal of service, especially in India and against the Boers. He was wounded at Majuba (p. 48 above) in 1881 and served with conspicuous gallantry under Roberts and Kitchener throughout the Boer War. As well as commanding in the field and at home, he held a succession of staff appointments and in 1909 became Adjutant-General. He was well qualified, it might be thought, to take a rational view of war, but being of a highly romantic temperament he was not immune from a cloudy exaltation which he expressed in the piece he wrote for Christopher Stone:

> As the Valkyrie ride exultant up northern skies to Valhalla, bearing fallen heroes home, spurning fear, pain and death beneath the hoof-strokes of their galloping horses, the President of the Peace Conference reclines in his opera-box - and yawns. The triumphant rush through the air; the clash of sword and hollow reverberating clang of brazen buckler, the storm and wild joy of battle are in his ears - but he hears not.[37]

Some seven or eight years later, this devotee of Nordic myth was to command at Gallipolli.

Politicians, as well as poets, novelists, soldiers and journalists, sometimes propagated a romantic view of war. Hugh Arnold-Foster MP (1855-1909), a grandson of Arnold of Rugby and Secretary for War under A J Balfour, wrote an introduction to *Peril and Patriotism,* a book for boys published in 1901. 'The days of chivalry', he said, 'with their romance and glitter ... are gone for ever. In our peaceful island ... we know nothing of the fierce excitement of war, the heroism, the horror, the peril, and the exhilaration of the battlefield.'[38]

In the face of this sort of writing, of which there was a good deal in the twenty years or so before 1914, it is difficult to maintain that the national mood was altogether peaceful. War and death in battle, on the contrary, were acquiring a romantic glamour uncomfortably similar to the glamour later ascribed to them by the Fascists and the Nazis. Romanticism of this kind focussed readily on the Empire, its wars and far-off battles, whether in the Sudan or on the North-West Frontier of India:

Take and break us: we are yours,
England, my own!
Life is good, and joy runs high
Between English earth and sky:
Death is death, but we shall die
To the Song on your bugles blown,
England-
To the stars on your bugles blown![39]

It was an emotion which, as feeling rose against Germany, could readily be
turned in that direction also.

IV

The Empire was not only something to die for. It was an ideal to live for. G.
S. Clarke (1848-1933), later Lord Sydenham of Combe, a technically
minded soldier who in 1900 was on a committee dealing with the
reorganisation of the War Office, spoke of 'the Empire, which to some of us
is almost a religion', and it might prompt on the one hand the arrogant
vaingloriousness which in the Diamond Jubilee year, 1897, made Kipling
pray:

For frantic boast and foolish word
Thy Mercy on Thy People, Lord!

On the other hand:

Take up the White Man's Burden -
Send forth the best ye breed -
Go bind your sons to exile
To serve your captives' need ...[40]

This latter sentiment, in the 1980's incomprehensible and derided, may
have been overstated, as Kipling overstated much. Nevertheless, alongside
the brassy unloveliness of some aspects of late Victorian imperialism, which
Kipling in some moods was much given to expressing, there was a sense of
mission which he also expressed and which informed much of the work
done by British soldiers and administrators overseas.

The numbers employed in governing the vast expanses of Queen
Victoria's Empire, particularly in the white colonies, were small and
scattered, strung round the world in places as different and as widely
separated as Gibraltar, British Guiana, Aden, Fiji and Swaziland. In British
India - that is, India outside the princely states, which covered a greater area
- there was the Indian Civil Service, open to Indians as well as Englishmen,
though not many were recruited. It was a remarkable group of men, highly
educated, selected by competitive examination, trained for government,

and about 1,100 strong. In the whole of India at the turn of the century there were about 75,000 British troops, a couple of thousand British officers with the Indian Army, and perhaps two or three thousand civil servants, police officers and other officials. The Anglo-Egyptian Sudan, after the reconquest, had the small, very select, Sudan Political Service. For the Empire as whole, there was no centrally organised Colonial Service until after the Great War. There were fifty or so colonial governors, each at the head of a rather sketchy civil administration, recruited on no settled plan, sometimes from barristers briefless in Britain, sometimes from army officers seeking greater pay, sometimes from young men of sound classical education but uncertain prospects. Much of the Empire was run by indirect rule: rule, that is, by local potentates under the eye of a British resident, perhaps with one or two British officers attached to local forces but without British administrators of any kind. The princely states of India were governed in this way. As for the armed forces, there were fewer than 120,000 Royal Navy and Royal Marines in 1901-2, and the peace-time strength of the army ran to about a quarter of a million, very widely dispersed.

Round the men who governed the Empire and fought its wars, especially the less exalted of them - the subalterns and captains, the district commissioners and assistant commissioners - the sahibs, the tuans, the effendis, the bwanas - Sanders of the River, Bones of the River - the legends and mystique of Empire gathered. It was they, although they were so few, who in the late Victorian world set a pattern for admiration at home and abroad of what an English gentleman (many of them were Scots or Irish) should be. Kipling described their work as he saw it in India and transferred the type backwards in English history in his Puck stories: his work sold in millions and still sells. 'These men of fair face and iron hand, just to the weak and swiftly merciless to the proud', said G. W. Steevens of 'the Sirdar [Kitchener] and their Excellencies', and again, describing a column of troops on the march, 'the officers were long-limbed, firmly knit, straight as lances. There are not many more pleasing sights in the world than the young British subaltern marching alongside his company ...'.[41]

To his heroes' gallery, at a lower social level, Kipling added the private soldier. In seventeen short stories scattered through Plain Tales from the Hills, Soldiers Three, Life's Handicap and Many Inventions, as well as the associated verse of Barrack Room Ballads and such pieces as 'Pharaoh and the Sergeant' in The Five Nations, he drew probably the most extended and certainly the best known character study of 'British Other Ranks' in English literature.

It was well timed. When Kipling began to write, the reputation of the

c

private soldier was tending upward, to some extent bcause of improved conditions of life. In the latter part of the 19th century, perhaps because of the influence of the public schools (Chapter Five below), officers began to take more interest than formerly in their men's welfare. They even went so far as to play football with them. During the same period flogging was abolished (1881) except on active service; short-service engagements were brought in; 'well-conducted' soldiers were allowed a month's furlough during the winter; living accomodation was improved. Flora Thompson (1877-1947), writing of rural Oxfordshire in her childhood, shows how it became possible for a young countryman to serve for a few years without committing social suicide, especially if he could get into the Royal Engineers or the Royal Artillery rather than the infantry.[42] Both were better paid than the infantry and service in a Telegraph Troop of the Royal Engineers provided training for skilled, secure civilian employment.

'Military service', says Edward M. Spiers, writing of the regular army in 1914, 'had a very limited appeal'[43], and he draws a dreary picture of the private soldier's life. On the other hand, at about that time Ward, Lock & Co., in *Our Soldiers and Sailors* and *The Wonder Book of Soldiers*, presented boys with a positively attractive vision of life in the ranks. No doubt they were helped by the army authorities, who themselves were glad of any help they could get with recruiting. In 1900 they allowed R. W. Paul (1869-1943) facilities for making a film - 'Army Life or How Soldiers are Made' - which was shown at the Alhambra Music Hall in London and was still on hire six years later,[44] and before 1914 they were employing professional advertising talent. Even when allowance is made for advertiser's licence, however, there is no reason to doubt that conditions of life for 'common soldiers' improved considerably during the forty years or so before 1914.

Apart from these material inducements, the rosy glow of public admiration, as imperial enthusiasm grew, began to play about the figure of the private soldier as it had long suffused the sailor. Alongside the idolised generals, Tommy Atkins emerged as a peculiarly British embodiment of the military virtues, just as Jack Tar had long symbolised the British bluejacket (and, it may be added, 'Bobby' symbolised the policeman: not, in most countries, an object of public affection). Tommy was always brave, always cheerful, formidable in battle yet chivalrous and sportsmanlike, always tender towards women and children. His faults were very much those of Henty's boys - a delight in challenging Authority to a not-too-serious conflict, with no hard feelings when Authority won. Altogether, a bit of a rascal, and all the more lovable for that. 'It was ... becoming the fashion', as one commentator says, 'to regard "Tommy Atkins" as a kind of domestic pet.'[45] How far fiction fitted the facts is not central to our purpose here.

What concerns us is that many people liked to believe in it.

Kipling's stories probably had a powerful influence. General Younghusband (p. 51 above), writing in 1917, went so far as to say 'Rudyard Kipling made the modern soldier'. Though sceptical of the truth of Kipling's creation, he thought soldiers modelled themselves on it.

> 'Other writers', Sir George continued, 'have gone on with the good work, and they between them have manufactured the cheery, devil-may-care, lovable person enshrined in our hearts as Thomas Atkins. Before he had learnt from reading stories about himself that he, as an individual, also possessed the above attributes, he was mostly ignorant of the fact. My early recollections of the British soldier [dating from 1878] are of a bluff, rather surly person, never the least jocose or light-hearted, except perhaps when he had too much beer. He was brave always, but with a sullen, stubborn bravery. No Tipperary ... about it.'[46]

By whatever agency, by 1914 all that was changed. The soldier was no longer the 'private of the Bluffs' (p. 42 above) who 'last night among his fellow roughs ... jested, quaffed and swore'. Low he might still rank in the social order, drunken on occasion, but he had become 'cheery, devil-may-care, lovable' Thomas Atkins.

He was the ultimate prop of the kind of life described in 1911 by Norah Watherston, whose husband, Lieutenant-Colonel A. E. G. Watherston (1867-1909), had recently been Commissioner of the Northern Territory of the Gold Coast. 'Five white people would assemble', wrote Mrs Watherston, 'in all the ceremony of mess-kit and medals, round a table that would not have disgraced any English home' - a quaint tribal custom to later, disapproving eyes, but in its day it symbolised both the isolation and the idealism of imperial service.
Mrs Watherston goes on:

> Surely it is not difficult to understand the fascination of walking into a country that is centuries behind the civilisation of Europe, with orders to bring that country into line with the rest of the world ... For, even if the people are a lower and dissimilar race, and although the soil is at the mercy of a ruthless climate, it is all new material, to be moulded for good or ill, and that moulding depends on the lives of Englishmen who serve England in her colonies.[47]

However incomprehensible or misguided it may have come to seem, there were in 1914 a great many Englishmen who were prepared to defend the ideal of Empire with their lives.

CHAPTER FOUR

Germany rising

I

Captain Owen Wheeler, writing for schoolboys in *Our Soldiers and Sailors* about 1912, explains:

> War, so far as Great Britain is concerned, may be divided into three classes: the very big war in which the interests of the whole nation, nay, of the whole Empire, are at stake; the moderately-sized war in which the country is seriously, but not quite vitally, concerned; and the "little war", which is usually undertaken for the purpose of punishing some small nation or tribe for an outrage upon British subjects or an insult to the British flag.[1]

During Queen Victoria's reign 'small nations or tribes' were punished frequently and the Indian Mutiny was ferociously put down, but there was no 'very big war' and only two of 'moderate size': against the Russians in the Crimea and against the Boers in South Africa. When the Victorians contemplated the possibility of a 'very big war', as they fairly frequently did, the enemies they expected, separately or together, were France and Russia, with Germany more likely an ally than an enemy. Sir Charles Dilke, for instance, writing in 1888, said: 'I shall ... mention only Russia and France as probable enemies, because ... Germany has no interests at variance with our own sufficiently important to be likely to lead to a quarrel.' A little further on he added: 'between ourselves and France differences are frequent, and between ourselves and Russia war is one day almost certain.'[2]

During the latter part of Queen Victoria's reign and the early years of the 20th century this position was totally reversed, until Germany became the most likely enemy and France - and even Russia - likely allies. The process has recently been studied from the broad diplomatic and political point of view by Paul M. Kennedy.[3] We are principally concerned to consider how, from the late 1890's onward, as war with Germany became year by year more likely, the state of feeling in Britain boiled up towards the highly volatile state it reached in 1914.

Quite why the French might have to be fought seems seldom to have been clearly thought out. For most people hostility to France was a habit of mind, not a logical conclusion, given some colour of credibility by rivalry in the Middle East, Egypt, and elsewhere. England and France had been enemies since the Middle Ages and it was taken for granted, on both sides of the Channel, that they always would be. With the Russians, the case was different. There were two clear grounds for hostility. First, the century-long Russian advance into Central Asia presented a permanent threat to the safety of British India. Secondly, the despotism of the Czars offended the nineteenth-century liberal mind.

Against the French the British were in the happy position, as they constantly reminded themselves, of having decisively won the long series of wars, almost uninterrupted from Marlborough's time until Wellington's, which ended with game, set and match at Waterloo. These wars, besides demonstrating to everyone's satisfaction the superiority of everything English over everything French, added Canada and several smaller territories to the British Empire and cleared the way for the conquest of India. They figure very prominently indeed in late Victorian patriotic writing, especially works aimed at the young.

Sir John Seeley (pp. 46-8 above) made great play with the eighteenth-century French wars in *The Expansion of England*. Nine of Fitchett's fifteen *Fights for the Flag* (p. 36 above) were against the French and they also provided the opposition for seventeen of his twenty-one *Deeds that won the Empire*. A list of Henty's heroes, far from complete, shows one *With Clive in India*, another *With Wolfe in Canada*, a third *Under Wellington's Command*, and a fourth *With Cochrane the Dauntless*, who 'scattered the French fleet in the Basque Roads'. The French wars were commemorated also in verse, much of it of a kind that lent itself to being learnt by heart and recited. Charles Moore's 'Burial of Sir John Moore' and Captain Marryatt's 'The Old Navy' ('The Captain stood on the carronade'), both written in the first half of the nineteenth century, wore well enough for Henley to include them in *Lyra Heroica* (p. 54 above) in 1891, along with Robert Browning's 'Home Thoughts from the Sea' ('Nobly, nobly, Cape St Vincent to the North-west dies away') which links victories over the Spanish (St Vincent, Cadiz, Gibraltar) with the battle of Trafalgar.

Apart from literature, no visitor to London could (or can) fail to be reminded, by Waterloo Bridge, Waterloo Road, Waterloo Station and Trafalgar Square, of Britain's two most famous victories over the French, and throughout the country portraits of Wellington and Nelson appeared on pub signs. The brief alliance with the French in the Crimea was not very readily remembered - the less so, perhaps, because the French were rather more successful there than the British - and Tennyson, in 1859, probably said what many others felt:

True, we have got *such* a faithful ally
That only the Devil can tell what he means.[4]

These two lines are from 'The War', best known for its refrain:

Form! Form! Riflemen form!
Ready, be ready to meet the storm!
Riflemen, riflemen, riflemen, form!

The poem was published in *The Times* on 9th May 1859, inspired by widespread excitement, almost amounting to panic, over a supposed threat of attack on England by Napoleon III. Feeling ran high enough in the early 1860's to bring about the formation of a Volunteer Force, revived and expanded from the Volunteers raised in the face of Napoleon I's invasion threat, of 150,000 men. At the same time the south and south-west coasts of England were elaborately fortified as far round as the Bristol Channel. To cover, presumably, the approaches to the South Wales ports and Bristol, seven-ton, seven-inch rifled cannon (RML MkIII) - the heaviest of their day - were emplaced on the promontory of Brean Down, on Steep Holm and Flat Holm in the Channel, and on the Glamorganshire shore. Many of them are still there.[5]

Victorian strategic planning, so far as it was concerned with Europe rather than with the Empire, always assumed that France would be the main enemy, especially at sea, where the French had the only fleet able to offer a serious threat to the Royal Navy. Whenever the Victorians had doubts about their ships, it was French ships that they compared them with; and the disposition of naval bases along the south and south-east coasts of England, with a powerful squadron in the Mediterranean, showed where danger was thought to be most likely. Also from the Mediterranean it was possible to watch and if necessary block Russian designs on Constantinople. In 1878 ships were ordered to Constantinople for that purpose, though in the end they did not go and it was achieved by other means.

In 1894 Alfred Harmsworth, for the first but by no means the last time in his career, addressed a work of imaginative fiction to the mass market which he was cultivating. He commissioned William Le Queux (1864-1927) to give lurid expression to his fears of the inadequacy of British defences in the face of foreign attack - naturally, from the French and Russians. Le Queux was in the early stages of a long and prolific career in light fiction, often with a 'spy' theme. Later on, in *Who's Who,* he claimed 'intimate knowledge of secret service of Continental powers.' For Harmsworth he wrote 'The Poisoned Bullet' to appear as a serial in *Answers* with appropriate quotations from retired admirals and generals alongside it.[6] Later the story appeared as a book, *The Great War in England* in 1897, which by the time 1897 arrived had gone into fourteen editions. From the ninth edition onward it was prefaced by a letter of comment from Lord Roberts.

Le Queux makes his war begin with a surprise declaration by the Russians. They are immediately joined by their allies the French. The *casus belli* has arisen from 'earnest negotiations between the Imperial Government [of Russia] and Great Britain for a durable pacification of Bosnia.' England is invaded. The Royal Navy, weak and inefficient, has been in large part mislaid - 'the Admiralty were unaware of the whereabouts of three whole Fleets' - and the country is rapidly overrun in spite of gallant feats of arms by the Volunteers. The brave Regulars are hampered by bad staff work and administrative arrangements which it was part of Le Queux's purpose to expose.[7]

The book is full of local colour which must have been the product of intensive research:

> In South Shields tragic scenes were being enacted .... The congested blocks of buildings around Panash Point were one huge furnace; the Custom House, the River Police Station, and the Plate Glass Works were wrecked, while a shell exploding in one of the petroleum tanks on the Commissioners' Wharf caused it to burst with fearful effect .... Amid this frightful panic, Lieut-Col Gowans and Major Carr of the 3rd Durham Artillery, the Mayor, Mr Readhead, Alderman Renoldson, Councillors Lisle, Marshall and Stainton, the Town Clerk, Mr Hayton, and the Rev. H E Savage, were all conspicuous for the coolness they displayed.[8]

No doubt these local worthies were gratified. It is to be hoped they were not embarrassed. Many other towns received similar treatment.

Help comes from three directions: from 'the legions of the Kaiser', from Italy, and from the colonies and India - 'the fate of England, nay, of our vast British Empire, was in the hands of those of her stalwart sons of many races who were now wielding valiantly the rifle and the sword.' Eventually all is well. The French are forced to cede Algeria and pay £250m indemnity. The Russians have to hand over vast territories in Central Asia. 'Dark days were succeeded by a period of happiness and rejoicing, and Britannia, grasping her trident again, seated herself on her shield beside the sea, Ruler of the Waves, Queen of Nations, and Empress of the World.'[9] From declaration to peace treaty, the war lasts from mid-August to mid-November: an expression of the orthodox view that no war between the Great Powers would last long.

Most of Le Queux's readers probably shared his confidence in spontaneous help from the colonies. His reliance on India might have been sceptically received in some circles, but no doubt by the 1890's, at least among the public at home, distrust of the sepoy army had been dispelled by the sentiments, not to say sentimentality, of end-of-the-century imperialism. The Queen certainly and many of her subjects probably had succumbed to the romantic spectacle of the Indian Army, that remarkable force of mercenaries which, in one form or another, upheld British power for the greater part of two centuries.

With Italy also there were sentimental ties, running back to the *Risorgimento*. Whether in the real world such considerations would have carried much weight seems doubtful. When the matter was put to the test in 1915 the Italians turned out to be hard bargainers.

The suggestion of help from Germany, presumably, looked plausible in 1894, even though anxiety in Britain about German industrial competition and about Prussian military strength was already keen. By 1897 a good deal of the plausibility must have been wearing off. Paul Kennedy regards the years between 1892 and 1895, when colonial and trade rivalries were growing sharper, as a watershed in Anglo-German relations.[10] These years ended in a festival of mutual hate set off early in 1896 by a telegram sent by the Kaiser to congratulate President Kruger on the failure of Dr Jameson's raid into the Transvaal in December 1895. It was a strong indication that Germany, in the minds of the British public, was beginning to appear as an enemy of the British Empire.

In looking at Germany the Victorians were accustomed to distinguishing between Prussians and the rest. They knew, respected and disliked Prussia: a power strong enough to brush Great Britain contemptuously aside in the attack on Denmark in 1863, to seize the leadership of Germany from Austria - and, in the process, to obliterate the Kingdom of Hanover, which took the Austrian side - in seven weeks in 1866 and then, having shattered the French Empire in less than a couple of months in 1870, to force the French into a humiliating peace early in 1871. The defeat of the French was thoroughly frightening, as the success of *The Battle of Dorking* by Colonel (later General Sir) G. T. Chesney (1830-95) showed. It was published anonymously in *Blackwood's Magazine* in 1871. It prompted twenty-three 'related works' and ran into five overseas editions and eight translations.[11] Its theme is a Prussian invasion of England against which England turns out to be defenceless.

Down to the time of the defeat of Napoleon III and the founding of the German Empire in 1871 most Germans seemed much less alarming than Prussian soldiers. They were fairly familiar in Britain, for until the influx of Russian Jews in the 1880's and 1890's they formed the largest immigrant community in the country. People thought of them, not very accurately, as slightly comic bandsmen and waiters, and as clerks who stole jobs by working for low wages: a complaint so persistent that the Census authorities twice investigated it, in 1881 and 1891, and twice dismissed it as unfounded.[12] Naturally they did not thereby kill it. Germans generally were identified with hard work and plain living; with immense erudition in recondite subjects; with excessive docility towards officials of an autocratic government; with music; with a certain visionary unpracticality. 'A learned German professor with blue spectacles', said a writer in 1899, referring to earlier opinion on the subject, 'was in our eyes more a subject of derision than of disquietude.'[13]

II

The blue-spectacled professors, the bandsmen, the waiters and the clerks were mostly subjects of small states whose main claim to distinction, and it was a very important one, was not military power but the excellence of their schools and universities. When these states were united under Prussian leadership in the German Empire, the superior British smile began to fade, because from the 1870's onward it became increasingly obvious that the Germans were challenging the British - and the Americans - for the industrial and commercial leadership of the world. Moreover they had a very good chance of success. The German Empire had excellent natural resources in coal and iron; a first-class educational system much more sensitive than the English, though possibly not the Scottish, system to the needs of industry; and a larger population (49 million in the German Empire against 37 million in the United Kingdom in 1890; by 1914 65 million against 45 million) with habits of work and discipline which were apt to fill British observers with wonder and apprehension.

The response to German economic rivalry was comparatively rational, but German rivalry was not wholly economic. It was also a matter of prestige. The Germans, like other European nations in the late nineteenth century, came to regard colonial possessions as desirable not only for reasons of trade but also as symbols of national success, as the indispensable appanages of a Great Power. This was very much the view of the emerging world order held by Dilke in the 1860's (p. 44 above) and by Seeley in the 1880's (p. 46 above). In 1898, when imperialist ambitions were at their height, not only in Great Britain but in Germany also, it was set out by Henry Birchenough (1853-1937: later a baronet). He was a prominent business man, a prolific writer, a member of numerous official committees and Royal Commissions. 'The future of the world belongs to great states,' he wrote in an article on the expansion of Germany in *The Nineteenth Century,* 'and ... a Germany without foreign possessions ... must necessarily dwindle in importance, in comparison with such world-states as Great Britain, Russia, the United States of America, and perhaps even France, are destined to become.'

Considerations of this sort were bound to bring Germany and Great Britain, the greatest imperial power of all, into a sphere of rivalry highly charged with emotion: the more so since Germany had started late in the search for territory. Birchenough went on:

The scramble among European nations for the remaining unappropriated portions of the earth's surface is at its height. Opportunities neglected now may never come again. The process of filling in ... the blanks upon the map is rapidly going on, and it is destined to determine, perhaps for centuries, the relative places which the nations of Europe will occupy in the world. Great Britain has already painted red huge patches of the map. France since the war of 1870 has splashed on her colour boldly and with unfaltering hand. Germany, under Bismarck, began to paint in her shade - somewhat tentatively at first - in the Cameroons, in South-West Africa, in East Africa, and in New Guinea.[14]

Nevertheless, as long as France and Russia were automatically thought of every time the enemies of Britain were mentioned, the rise of Germany was not seen by everyone in Britain or the British Empire as an inevitable cause of conflict. Rather, indeed, the reverse, as Le Queux's book suggests. Given the prevailing racial theories of the late 1890's, Great Britain and Germany, rivals in business though they might be, looked to many people more like natural allies, preferably with the addition of the United States, than like enemies.

Among those who took this view at this time were Alfred and Harold Harmsworth, Cecil Rhodes and Joseph Chamberlain. To them an alliance between the 'Anglo-Saxon Powers' - the British Empire and the United States - and the rising Teutonic Power, Germany, looked very attractive. 'Both England and the United States are civilising Powers', ran a *Daily Mail* leader in 1898. 'In no distant future they may have to stand shoulder to shoulder with Germany against the half-barbarous Power [Russia] that now threatens Europe.' H. M. Stanley (1841-1904), the African explorer, in the same year, went so far as to suggest that Great Britain should join or at least favour the Triple Alliance of Germany, Austria-Hungary and Italy:

The Triple Alliance supported by the military and naval strength of Great Britain, backed by the moral support of the United States, and by the military and naval forces of Japan, appears to me the only way by which the peace of the world can be secured, this nightmare of war dispelled, and the eternal agitation [by Russia and France] effectually stopped.[15]

Cecil Rhodes died in 1902. He left endowments for about 170 scholarships to be held at Oxford by 'Rhodes scholars' from the colonies, the United States (which Seeley called 'almost as good as a colony') and Germany. Joseph Chamberlain, in 1899, called for 'a triple alliance of the Teutonic race' between Great Britain, Germany and the USA.[16]

Chamberlain's proposal was badly received in all the countries concerned. By the time he made it Germany had begun to emerge decisively as an enemy of Great Britain, for the Kaiser's Government had committed itself to building a powerful battle fleet. To the existing seven German battleships, two large cruisers and ten light cruisers, the Navy Law of April 1898 proposed to add, within six years, twelve battleships, ten large cruisers and twenty-three smaller ones.[17] No policy could have been better calculated to alarm and irritate the British.

That the Navy Law of 1898 was directed against Great Britain is certain.[18] Did it represent a reasonable policy for a German government to follow? The British argued that Germany was the strongest European power on land as Great Britain was at sea, and that adding naval strength to military strength was needlessly provocative, adding nothing to Germany's power against her declared enemies, France and Russia. The German answer was partly that Germany's growing trade and colonial empire needed naval protection, just as British trade and the British Empire did, and partly that there was a danger of a British descent on the German Baltic coast. Was there any such danger? The possibility was in the mind of Admiral Fisher, First Sea Lord from 1904-10 and again in 1914-5, for as long as he held office, and in the past the British fleet had been used aggressively in Northern waters at Copenhagen in 1801 and at Walcheren in 1809.[19]

From 1898 the Royal Navy and the Imperial German Navy were built up in conscious rivalry. Guns grew rapidly larger, armour heavier, engines more powerful; and the 'naval race' was a matter not only of more but also of better, for a major advance in design such as HMS *Dreadnought,* 1906, put every other capital ship on the other side at risk. It was all very good for trade, for apart from the demand from the Admiralty there was a flourishing export business. In 1914 twelve capital ships were building in British yards for the Royal Navy and foreign navies, besides the numerous smaller vessels needed for a balanced fleet. Shipbuilding and heavy engineering throve, with naval work taking up the slack when orders for merchant ships fell off. In the early years of the twentieth century most of the world's ocean-going ships were built in the United Kingdom, especially on the Clyde, and Glasgow has never been so prosperous since. All the time long lines of massively sinister ships, 'like giants bowed in anxious thought',[20] gave solid embodiment to the immense charge of ill-will, fear, pride and suspicion which was building up between Great Britain and Germany.

At the level of high policy, relations between Great Britain and Germany during the last fifteen years or so before the Great War varied from moderately good to extremely bad. The two powers co-operated in a blockade of Venezuela in 1902 but were twice, perhaps three times, close to war - in 1906 and 1911 over affairs in North Africa and in 1908-9 over a

Balkan crisis in some ways similar to the Balkan crisis which precipitated the Great War in 1914. Meanwhile Great Britain's relations with her old enemies France and Russia, which were also Germany's enemies, were put on a friendly footing by the Entente Cordiale with France in 1904 and the Anglo-Russian Convention of 1907. Gradually a Triple Entente - Great Britain, France, Russia - emerged in opposition to the Triple Alliance - Germany, Austria-Hungary, Italy. Gradually, hazily, uncertainly, the battle-lines of 1914-18 were drawn.

High policy is less our concern than popular feeling: complex, highly emotional, sometimes self-contradictory. Its leading theme, often and stridently proclaimed, was that the Germans intended to attack the British Empire from motives of envy, greed and ambition. D. C. Boulger (1853-1928), an eminent journalist and author with a special interest in Turkey, Egypt, India and China, writing in 1906 in the sober *Nineteenth Century,* asserted: 'If a German ruler ever holds "the trident" we shall become a German colony.' That the Germans might have equal and opposite suspicions was a less popular point of view, usually associated with radical political opinions. Lord Avebury (1834-1913), a Liberal, replied to Boulger:

> The Germans ... ask themselves why we have so enormously increased our Army and Navy. ... They observe the *entente cordiale* with France, they know we are not going to attack Russia or the United States, and it is not suprising that they should have suspected that these "bloated armaments" ... were directed against them.[21]

In 1903 Erskine Childers followed his successful *In the Ranks of the CIV* with *The Riddle of the Sands,* in which two Englishmen use a yachting holiday to penetrate a German plan for an invasion of England launched from the shallow waters off East Friesland, which Childers knew from yachting excursions of his own. The writing is so vivid, the details of geography and seamanship are so exact, that the book carries conviction through instilling a suspicion that it may not be entirely fictitious. Before 1914 it went through ten impressions and 73 years later it was in print in four editions.

Childers, educated at Haileybury and Trinity College Cambridge, became a clerk in the House of Commons, a dignified and at that time not over-strenuous occupation, from which he departed for his few months' service in South Africa and to which he returned. He served with distinction in the Great War.[22] By birth, education, occupation he belonged to the upper middle class of Victorian England: the class which provided the professioal men, politicians, serious journalists and writers on current affairs, army and navy officers, civil servants at home and in the empire, dons and public-school masters and others whose ideas and attitudes were dominant in England in their day. Of these ideas and attitudes Childers, when he wrote *The Riddle of the Sands,* was a convinced exponent. *The Riddle of the Sands,* especially read with *In the Ranks of the CIV,* conveys an atmosphere of romantic and warlike patriotism, ardent and innocent. It opens a window into the pre-1914 mentality at an influential level in society, adding to the impressions gained from Kipling, Henty, Churchill, Steevens.

Both Childers' books are set in the days when, in Professor Medlicott's penetrating phrase, 'it was fun to be an Englishman'[23], especially in the upper orders of society. In those days 'clubland heroes', the free-lance adventurers created before and after the Great War by Rider Haggard, John Buchan, 'Sapper' (H. C. McNeile), 'Dornford Yates' (C. W. Mercer) and other authors were not immeasurably far removed from the truth.[24] In *The Riddle of the Sands* the narrator, Carruthers, is a clerk in the Foreign Office - that is, a first-division civil servant - much as Childers was a clerk in the House of Commons. His hours of work are short and he can take a great deal of leave. He speaks of spending several weeks in Germany after his cruise, which itself lasts at least four weeks. There is no hindrance to travel - no passports needed - and the sovereign passes current everywhere.

It is the period, too, of the gifted amateur, when an Englishman of the right upbringing and education could do anything if he set his mind to it. Carruthers and his companion Davies - the two of them are perhaps a composite self-portrait of Childers - set their minds towards espionage. Amateur spying was far from being a novelist's invention. Army officers in real life were discreetly encouraged to engage in it. Among those who did were Captain F. W. Burnaby (1842-85), who rode to Khiva in 1875 in defiance of the Russian authorities, and Captain R. S. S. Baden-Powell, who also spied on the Russians a little later.[25] In 1910 Captain B. F. Trench of the Royal Marines was sentenced to four years in a German fortress for espionage. In the following year a well-connected London solicitor, Bertrand Stewart, was in trouble for cruising in Frisian waters (the location of *The Riddle of the Sands*: can the coincidence have been accidental?) and trying to gain information about the defences of the East Frisian islands and the Weser estuary.[26] Both Trench and Stewart had accomplices. Evidently spying was yet another form of sport for adventurous English gentlemen and it seems to have been regarded with surprising tolerance in Imperial Germany.

Childers did not seek to promote hatred of the Germans. Those whom he brings into his narrative are affectionately described, the villain is a traitorous English naval officer, and Davies and Carruthers speak admiringly of the Kaiser and his works. 'Isn't it splendid?' says Davies of the Kiel Canal, and then: 'he's a fine fellow, that Emperor.' Carruthers sketches the rise of imperial Germany in glowing terms. Davies, the more simple-minded of the two, responds:

> He [Davies] used to listen rapt while I [Carruthers] decribed her marvellous awakening in the last generation, under the strength and wisdom of her rulers; her intense patriotic ardour; her seething industrial activity, and, most potent of all the forces that are moulding modern Europe, her dream of a Colonial Empire, entailing her transformation from a land-power to a sea-power. ... "And we aren't ready for her," Davies would say; "we don't look her way. We have no naval base in the North Sea, and no North Sea Fleet. ... And suppose she collars Holland, isn't there some talk of that? ... I don't blame them: the Rhine ceases to be German just when it begins to be most valuable. ... We can't talk about conquest and grabbing. We've collared a fine share of the world, and they've every right to be jealous.[27]

The mingled hostility and admiration displayed in this passage - hostility to German intentions, admiration for German achievement - was widespread, as perhaps a converse sentiment may have been in Germany. Germany, as an industrial and colonial power, was so similar in many ways to Great Britain, and the racial connexion between the two nations was so widely recognised, that Germany was often held up in Great Britain as an object lesson, usually for the purpose of drawing disquieting conclusions. In the view of P. A. Hislam in 1908:

> Germany is virile, England is lethargic; Germany is aggressive, England is peaceful; Germany is ambitious, England is complacent. The temperament of the two peoples promises nothing with more certainty than that when Germany believes her opportunity to have come she will have no difficulty in taking England unawares. Not only does our national frame of mind offer a great temptation to an eager and expansive people, but it is Germany's only chance.[28]

From this point it was not far to go to predicting national degeneration and decline: a prediction which came all the more easily because classical education prompted comparison between Great Britain and Rome. 'The main cause of the downfall of Rome', wrote Baden-Powell, as an historian both confident and unreliable but nonetheless an influential public figure, 'was the decline of good citizenship ... due to want of energetic patriotism, to the growth of luxury and idleness, and to the exaggerated importance of local party politics etc.' He detected the same causes of downfall in Great Britain in 1907. These remarks were not linked directly to the German menace but he believed in it. 'Germany', he said in 1908, 'wants to develop her trade and commerce and must therefore get rid of England.'[29] His economics were as shaky as his history. Britain and Germany were extremely valuable to each other as trading partners, but that fact escaped him, as it escaped many observers of Anglo-German relations in each country.

III

In the last half-dozen years before 1914, feeling in Britain against Germany was excitable and more than once rose to a pitch bordering on panic, especially during the naval scare of 1908-9 - 'We want eight [dreadnoughts] and we won't wait' - and the Agadir crisis of 1911, when the two nations came close to war. The circulation of the *Daily Mail* was now about 750,000 and since 1900 other papers had come into the mass market as well, such as C. A. Pearson's *Daily Express,* launched in 1900, Alfred Harmsworth's *Daily Mirror* (1903) and Horatio Bottomley's weekly *John Bull* (1906). By 1900 Alfred Harmsworth, reversing his former opinions, began to foresee war with Germany, and the *Mail* gave expression to his views.[30]

With the encouragement of Harmsworth and the enthusiastic assistance of William Le Queux, E. Phillips Oppenheim (1866-1946) and other imaginative writers, a 'spy-scare' was built up, from about 1908 onwards, which seems to have had no rational basis whatever. A very large network of secret agents was supposed to exist. Germans living in England - clerks, waiters, musicians and others - were seen as trained soldiers who would rise to assist an invading army, especially by demolition and sabotage. The most innocent activities of German visitors, especially if they were seen to be looking at maps and writing notes, were given the most sinister interpretation.[31]

The kind of people who read the organs of educated opinion, Christopher Andrew makes clear, were thoroughly taken in by the spy stories. They were not, however, pleased by the success of the *Daily Mail*. 'Written by office boys for office boys', Lord Salisbury is reported to have said. Sir Robert Ensor (1877-1958), quoting the remark about forty years after it was made, displayed equally lofty contempt for Alfred Harmsworth, his intentions, his methods, his papers and his imitators. He 'was identified by his Radical critics', says Professor A. J. A. Morris, perhaps the most recent and certainly one of the most authoritative of them, 'as the greatest scaremonger in the British press, a title he accepted ... with alacrity.'[32] A contributor to *Punch* accused the 'yellow press' of deliberately fomenting war,[33] and in general the pre-1914 popular papers have been charged with irresponsible sensationalism to which their more serious contemporaries would not descend.

There was certainly plenty of sensationalism about. It can seen in contributions to *The Nineteenth Century,* in the works of Rudyard Kipling, in *The Riddle of the Sands,* and it would be easy to find much more. It found visual accompaniment in the cartoon style of the period. In the pages of *Punch* Sir John Tenniel (1820-1914), E. L. Sambourne (1844-1910), Bernard Partridge (1861-1945), L. Raven-Hill (1867-1942) and others paraded the Great Powers through a fantasy world inhabited by buxom allegorical ladies (Europa, Germania, Peace, Marianne, Britannia and others as required), a zooful of animals (the British bulldog, the Russian bear, the Gallic cock), and strangely dressed gentlemen, principally Uncle Sam, lean, stringy, sardonic, and John Bull, middle-aged, middle-class, testy, over-weight, wearing clothes a hundred years out of date. It is probably significant that John Bull's clothes are roughly those of the period of England's greatest glory as a European power, just after the defeat of Napoleon.

If this was the content of much of the 'serious' press, it is difficult to see what cause of complaint lay against the *Daily Mail* and its competitors. Their layout was restrained, their language at least as dignified, not to say pompous, as the language of those who sneered at them. Contributors to the *Mail,* attracted by high fees, were often people who also wrote at the 'heavy' end of the market. The *Daily Mail's* news coverage was wide. What was said was said with force and clarity. It carried much the same message as a considerable part of the 'serious' press was carrying: that Germany was a menace, that Britain was decadent, that more and more men should be trained to arms, and so on.

Perhaps the *Daily Mail's* most celebrated set-piece of scaremongery was the series of articles which it commissioned towards the end of 1909 from Robert Blatchford (1851-1943), once a sergeant of the 103rd Foot, who had founded a socialist weekly, the *Clarion,* in 1891 and then fallen out with other socialists over his support for the Boer War. He visited Germany and wrote ten articles, published between 13th and 23rd December 1909, which were revised and reprinted immediately after war broke out in August 1914 as a pamphlet under the title *The War that was Foretold,* which perhaps sufficiently indicates their general tenor. The sensation they created, both in Germany and Great Britain, appears to have been all that Northcliffe could desire[34]

Horatio Bottomley's style may be judged from two articles published in *John Bull* in December 1911, after the Agadir crisis, under the title 'Germany must be Stopped!' They rehearsed the familiar British view of

German strength, policy and institutions, especially in colonial and naval matters, and suggested 'it is natural that Germany should desire to annex Belgium, and even Holland'. 'In our opinion', the editor concluded, 'war is inevitable - and Sir Edward Grey [the Foreign Secretary] knows it', but the editor thought it unlikely that Germany would attack until her navy was much stronger and the Kiel Canal had been widened to take the largest ships. Therefore 'we must strike whilst we are in a favourable position.'[35] The British Government, that is, was being advised to confirm the Germans' darkest suspicions.

This is 'yellow journalism' at its most inflammatory, but its general substance - that war with Germany was coming and what later came to be called a 'pre-emptive strike' might be desirable - can be found at higher and professedly more respectable levels. In 1906 the Earl of Erroll (1841-1927) had forecast in The Nineteenth Century a German invasion of Belgium.[36] It had been foreseen as far back as 1888 by Sir Charles Dilke, 'but in my belief', he had said, 'the British public are not willing to fight in defence of Belgium.'[37] Sir John Fisher, First Sea Lord, calculated in 1906 that the Germans would need eight years - until 1914 - to rebuild the Kiel Canal. They would then get their harvest in and go to war, probably at a Bank Holiday. Fisher thought the British Government should strike first. The Germans, for their part, were determined, if war broke out in Europe, to move on France, and in 1905 General Count von Schlieffen (1833-1913), before his retirement as Chief of the German General Staff, had prepared the plan for an attack through Belgium which was carried out in 1914.[38]

What the organs of the 'yellow press' said, then, did not differ much from what was said in more august circles, but their wide circulation carried knowledge of public affairs and comment upon them much further than ever before. On that knowledge, on that comment, a great many people, including men of military age, must have formed such opinions as they had. Whether such opinions were justified is not at issue here. What concerns us is that in the increasingly feverish atmosphere of early twentieth-century Europe the English popular papers - papers of a new kind, very recently developed - added their considerable power to the tide which was sweeping the nation, perhaps not altogether against its will, closer and closer to war.

IV

From the turn of the century onward belief that the Germans were preparing an attack led directly to a movement for compulsory military service, a notion repellent to the Victorian liberal mind and especially unpopular among the working classes. It might have been even more unpopular if people had known that as late as 1891 the Secretary of State for War, defining 'the objects of our military organisation', had placed at the head of his list: 'The effective support of the civil power in all parts of the United Kingdom'.[39]

Part of Childers' object in writing *The Riddle of the Sands* was to put the case for compulsory service. 'Is it not becoming patent', he asks in the final sentence of the book, 'that the time has come for training all Englishmen systematically either for the sea or for the rifle?' Lord Roberts, the nation's favourite general, took up the cause enthusiastically and in 1905 became President of the National Service League, a body formed in 1902 to press for universal military training. Alongside it the Navy League, founded in 1894, existed to spread information about the navy and insist upon its paramount importance for the safety and peace of the nation. In Childers' terms, both 'the rifle' and 'the sea' thus had their propagandist organisations. The *National Review,* owned and edited by L. J. Maxse (1864-1932), an Admiral's son and a talented writer, was always in favour of compulsory service.[4]

The National Service League found support among those who believed that military training inculcated most of the virtues desirable in a good citizen, which were apt to be virtues which the middle class deplored the absence of in the working class. In 1905 the directors of Joseph Crosfield & Sons, a large Lancashire soap firm, said in a brochure:

> The Directors, Managers, Foremen and a large number of the men are members and ardent supporters of the National Service League, being convinced that Universal National Service is very desirable in the interest of all manufacturers as it would improve the nation physically and mentally and create and develop in all classes a desire to serve the community.[41]

The directors' support for the idea of compulsory service we need not doubt. It is an idea which always commends itself more strongly to the middle-aged than to the young. The 'large number of men' no doubt found it politic to agree with their employers.

Resistance to the idea of compulsion could readily be taken as evidence of the national degeneracy so widely feared. Neither foreigners nor colonials were so base as to expect, as Englishmen did, to avoid fighting by paying professionals to do it for them. 'From Paris to Pretoria, and from Archangel to Auckland, the private citizen is under bond to shed his blood for his country; in Great Britain alone he sheds nothing but his money, and pays a body of professional troops to discharge his patriotic duties for him.' That was written in 1899. A dozen years later the tone was more feverish: 'Why is it that now ... the whole Anglo-Saxon race, alike in the British Empire and in the United States, is in visible danger of overthrow?' The suggested answer foreshadows a pronouncement, in the years between the wars, by Benito Mussolini: 'Because their women shrink from motherhood and their men from the practice of arms.'[42]

H. H. Munro (1870-1916) - 'Saki', the satirist of Edwardian fashionable society - developed the theme of decadence and distaste for military service in *When William Came,* published in 1914. William is the Kaiser. The book displays the same hard, epigrammatic brilliance as the author's short stories. It describes the results of a German invasion of England launched and completed between a Saturday and a Friday. Munro's political tendencies would in the 1980's be described as 'fascist'. Like Childers in *The Riddle of the Sands,* he presents the Germans in a favourable, rather admiring light. They have obviously fought in a most civilised way, and the occupation of Great Britain is gentlemanly. There seem to be no restraints on personal freedom more serious than a ban on walking on the grass in parks and on bearing arms, but that is something no one wants to do. Travellers pass freely in and out of the country and the London social round goes on undisturbed by anything so barbarous as a resistance movement. In Delhi King George V, Emperor of India, reigns over the British Empire, which outside the United Kingdom has survived intact.

The book is a protest against the luxury-loving, easy-going life of the leisured class in pre-war England and against the 'apathy' of the working class. The general self-indulgence and apathy among all classes has made compulsory service impossible, and the result has been the downfall and occupation of Great Britain. Munro disliked the working class only slightly less than he disliked the Jews. He assumed, in accordance with socialist theory, that class interests were considered more important by working men than national interests. They had therefore 'indirectly, a greater share of the responsibility, because the voting power was in their hands ... their own industrial warfare was more real to them than anything that was threatening them from the nation they only knew from samples of German clerks and German waiters.'[43]

The guiltiness with which Munro and many others in the upper levels of society regarded the ease and luxury of their lives provided a strong motive for them to respond eagerly to the challenge of war when it came:

Now, God be thanked Who has matched us with His hour,
And caught our youth, and wakened us from sleeping ...[44]

Thus Rupert Brooke in 1914. Munro was forty-four years old in that year and could with perfect honour have stayed at home. He joined the army, refused a commission, and was killed in 1916.

Among those who deplored the national decadence was Sir Robert Baden-Powell, and his remedy for it lay in the Boy Scout movement which he started with a camp on Brownsea Island, in Poole Harbour, in 1907. Horatio Bottomley was unflattering. 'General Baden-Powell's latest attempt at advertisement', said *John Bull* on 25th January 1908, 'is to organise a corps of boy scouts', and the article went on to ridicule it. Baden-Powell was a master of self-advertisement and Boy Scouts have always had their ridiculous side. At the same time, the instant, lasting and eventually international success of scouting showed that if it was a joke, it was a good joke and a durable one.

Baden-Powell was a general. His movement was inspired by the way he had employed boys during his most celebrated military achievement, the defence of Mafeking, the Boer War episode on which his enormous popularity was chiefly based. He used that popularity to get his movement going - it could hardly have succeeded so rapidly otherwise. In spite of this military aura, Baden-Powell always maintained, and there is no reason to doubt his sincerity, that no military intention underlay scouting. 'Remember ...', he wrote in *Scouting for Boys,* 'that a Scout is not only a friend to the people round him, but "a friend to all the world". Friends don't fight each other.'[45]

By contrast, the Boys' Brigade, founded in 1883 in Glasgow by Sir William Alexander Smith (1854-1914), an enthusiastic officer of Volunteers, was avowedly military in its inspiration and gave a prominent place to drill in its activities, aimed at working-class boys in the great cities. By 1914 the Boys' Brigade had about 150,000 members and alongside it were the Church Lads' Brigade, the Boys' Life Brigade, the Catholic and the Jewish Brigades. They managed to combine religious and military inspiration in a manner thoroughly charcteristic of the age. 'These Brigades', said an admiring commentator just before 1914, writing in *The Wonder Book of Soldiers,* 'have made a difference already in the great cities, and they will make a still greater change when all the present members have become citizens.'[46]

'B.-P.', notwithstanding his denial of military motives, was nevertheless an orthodox patriotic imperialist, and his movement took its tone from him and from the times. 'I suppose', he wrote in the opening sentence of *Scouting for Boys,* 'every boy wants to help his country in some way or other. There is a way by which he can do so easily, and that is by becoming a Boy Scout.' The founder may not have intended any military significance to be read into remarks like this, but plenty of other people found it. Scouting was just the sort of movement, with mass rallies, singing, camping, private ritual, group loyalties and discipline, which might have been deliberately set up to cultivate the bellicose patriotism which many people considered the country needed in its young men.

THE EMPIRE'S HOPE, said a headline in the *Daily Express* of 5th July 1911. VAST ARMY OF BOY SCOUTS REVIEWED BY THE KING - ROYAL MESSAGE APPRECIATION OF A GREAT WORK. 'The great lack of the mass of our people', said the text under the headlines, 'is discipline. We have nothing to do for us what universal military training does for our neighbours.' Ward, Lock & Co., publishers, certainly saw a link between the Scouts and the armed services for in *Our Soldiers and Sailors* and the very successful *Wonder Book of Soldiers* which replaced it they included a tale called 'The Stranger and the Scouts'.[46]

The Stranger is 'a tall bronzed soldierly man' who 'can't feel at home in your big cities.' He meets the narrator on Hampstead Heath, sees a patrol of scouts, and remarks 'it is some years since I was in England ... and many things are new to me. I wish I took to all the new things as much as I take to the cut of those youngsters.' The narrator gives a highly approving account of the scouts and their founder - and of the Boys' Brigade and their founder, too - and the Stranger concludes 'There's hope for the Old Country yet ... when these boys are men, things are going to be different, so long as they keep the Scout Law, or the aims of their Brigades.' In *Our Soldiers and Sailors* the story is accompanied by a coloured plate, 'Cheering the Chief Scout', in which the Union Flag is prominent, as it was in scout camps. There is no direct mention of military service, but strong insistence on patriotism, and by 1914 many boys must have acquired from scouting - and from the Boys' Brigades - an outlook which made volunteering in 1914 seem the most natural thing in the world to do.

Voluntary enlistment, for many professional soldiers, remained preferable to compulsion. In 1910 Ian Hamilton, then Adjutant-General, was not merely permitted but encouraged to publish an official memorandum, *Compulsory Service,* which did not favour it at all. Other influential (and middle-aged) figures did. Conan Doyle, at the time of the Boer War, wanted 'to extend the Militia Act for short periods of home service.' About 1908 or a little earlier Rudyard Kipling, in 'The Army of a Dream', set out an impenetrably elaborate scheme which reads as if it would have turned the entire country into an armed camp.[47] Notwithstanding all the pressure brought to bear and the prestige of Lord Roberts, too, compulsory service never came within the scope of practical politics in pre-1914 Britain. Aversion to it ran wide and deep and, with the English Channel as a moat commanded by the navy, there was no very obvious reason, in spite of frequent invasion scares, why the voluntary principle should not be applied to defence as well as to other public activities.

It was applied differently, nevertheless, to the regular forces and to the Volunteers. In the regular forces only officers could be said to serve on a truly voluntary basis, in the sense that an officer joined of his own free will and could resign his commission if he wished. For the man in the ranks it was only the act of enlistment that was voluntary. After that he would be held rigidly to service for a term of years with the colours and a further term on the reserve, unless as an act of favour he was allowed to 'buy himself out': a process too expensive for most soldiers or their families to contemplate.

The Volunteers were described accurately enough by their title. Authority over them could be exercised only in so far as they accepted it, and for most purposes they were members of a club, often with little to distinguish the officers socially from the men. Membership of the club might be quite expensive, especially for officers. General Hamley, in 1889, wrote of volunteers buying extra ammunition, paying some of their travelling expenses, subscribing towards the maintenance of their corps. One commanding officer told Hamley that he had spent several thousands out of his own pocket on his corps, 'which he can no longer continue to do'.[48]

The 'club' atmosphere and the corresponding expenditure reached its height in Yeomanry regiments: cavalry units with a strong 'county' flavour, distinct from the general run of Volunteers. The men provided their own horses and a 'contingent allowance' of £2 per efficient man rarely met the cost of uniforms, band, horses for the permanent staff, and other items. 'The esprit de corps of the Yeomanry', wrote Colonel Dunlop of the period before 1914, 'was very high, but ... it tended to centre on the locality and the commanding officer rather than on the Army as a whole or the War Office in particular.'[49]

When the Volunteer Force was reconstructed in the 1860's it also ostentatiously avoided identification with the regulars by serving without pay and wearing uniforms of strikingly non-uniform design and of any colour but scarlet. Moreover it drew recruits from classes that did not send men to the regulars. 'I do not believe', said a Scottish Volunteer colonel in 1862, 'that a single man in my regiment would have enlisted either into the militia or into the regular army; they are of the class of mechanics, and not of the class that generally enlist.'[50] There was a strong middle-class element in the Volunteers and Col Dunlop goes so far as to call them 'fundamentally a movement of the rapidly rising Victorian professional and middle classes.'[51]

Employers were inclined to look on the Volunteers with favour, for much the same reasons as some of them supported compulsory service. 'A Company of the 1st Volunteer Battalion (PWV) South Lancashire

Regiment', said Crosfields' directors in 1905, 'is furnished exclusively by the Works.' The firm's managers were encouraged to become Volunteer officers and every Volunteer was allowed a fortnight at camp each year, the firm paying one full week's wages and the difference between regimental pay and the man's wages for another week. An hour's drill a week was allowed in the firm's time.[52]

Perhaps as a result of this kind of encouragement, perhaps for other reasons - rifle-shooting? patriotism? a desire to stand well with the boss? - men of the working class joined the Volunteer Force in sufficient numbers, by the early twentieth century, to provide about 75 per cent of its strength.[53] By that time the Volunteers had been brought into rather closer contact with the regulars. In 1908 there were nearly 266,000 Volunteers and Yeomanry, about 100,000 below establishment.[54] With the men who had previously passed through the Volunteers, there must have been half a million men or so, outside the regulars and the militia, who had had some sort of training in arms. In spite of the opposition to compulsion, it appears that military service, on the easy terms offered by the Volunteers, was a fairly strong minority taste.

Not strong enough, however, to satisfy all observers. Some made disapproving comparisons with the national taste for sport. Major-General Sir Alex B. Tulloch (1838-1920), elderly and distinguished, asserted in 1906:

> In Germany and far-distant Japan, to undergo the necessary training for making a man capable of defending his country, and being ready to die for it, is an almost sacred duty. Here, however, looking on at a football or cricket match where professionals are playing is much more to the taste of British youth, tens of thousands of whom idle their spare time away rather than join even the Volunteers, who so patriotically try to do their duty.[55]

Kipling, a few years earlier, had made the same point with his often-quoted attack on 'the flannelled fools at the wicket ... and the muddied oafs at the goals.' He was himself hopelessly incompetent at ball games, which may have influenced his outlook. He also enquired ironically of those who enjoyed shooting:

> Will the rabbit war with your foemen - the red deer horn them for hire?
> Your kept cock pheasant keep you? - he is master of many a shire.[56]

It is just as well that the Volunteers never had to face an invading force. Unlike the regular, the volunteer could indulge his taste for military life as he pleased and for as long as he pleased, and that even applied to service in South Africa. As late as the Second World War, Territorial Army troops from Ulster were sent home from Burma when the period of their engagement for foreign service ran out, much to the amazement and irritation of other British troops whose terms of service were less favourable.[57]

Although, in the view of a recent student of the Volunteers, they did something to raise the reputation of the regulars,[58] the regulars' view of the Volunteers, understandably, was not high, and when Kitchener came to the War Office in 1914 he brought with him deep contempt for all amateur soldiers. It was not, however, the Volunteers on whom he vented it, but the Territorial Force, which replaced the Volunteers in 1908.

It was a force modelled much more closely on the regular army and much more closely linked with it, because the Secretary for War who created it - R. B. Haldane (1856-1928, later Lord Haldane of Cloan) - intended it not as a haphazard collection of miscellaneous troops for local defence but as a second line to the Expeditionary Force which would be required when - rather than if - war broke out with Germany.[59] A leader in the *Daily Mail* on 1st April 1908 observed:

> The Territorial Force to-day rises phoenix-like from the ashes of the Volunteer Force and begins a career which all patriotic men trust may prove one of brilliant success. ... It is now the plain duty of every patriotic citizen to exert himself to the utmost for the success of this great experiment. If it fails, which fortune forbid, then universal service becomes necessary and inevitable.

Behind the Volunteers and the Yeomanry were strong local loyalties. 'To break with tradition', as Haldane observed,[60] 'and weld their substance into something quite novel was likely to be a very serious undertaking.' He approached it by basing the new Force on County Associations (hence the curious title 'Territorial'), by reviving the archaic but evocative county office of Lord Lieutenant and by giving the gentry a large part to play. Nevertheless there was a good deal of doubt about how many Volunteers would transfer to the new force. *John Bull* on 23rd May 1908 prophesied failure. The same paper, on 26th August 1911, criticised 'some Territorial officers ... Army failures for the most part.' Critics, especially advocates of compulsory service, were never silent, and one of the contributors to *The Times History of the War,* writing probably in 1915, considered that hostile criticism 'from first to last ... almost controlled the recruiting.'[61]

The Territorial Force, therefore, had in its early days 'a troubled history'.[62] The strength of the Territorial Force at the end of 1908 was only 188,000,[63] well below the strength of the old Volunteer Force. The Territorials reached 276,000 at the beginning of 1910, but they never reached their peace establishment of about 314,000. In 1913 about 66 per cent of 'Terriers' went to camp for fifteen days - the most important feature of the year's training - and 23 per cent attended more briefly.[64] By the time war broke out numbers had fallen. There were only about 250,000 Territorials, some 200,000 fewer than the regulars and their reserves.[65] Thus, hesitantly, the foundations were laid of the non-professional armies, some $5\frac{1}{2}$ million strong, which were raised in Great Britain during the Great War. On 4th August 1914 the only element in those armies which was in existence was the Territorial Force.

CHAPTER FIVE

The temples of the faith: 'the best school of all'

The public schools were at the height of their prestige and influence during the forty years or so before the Great War.[1] This was the period of imperial glory when the prestige of England - with which the rest of the United Kingdom was in most minds, British and foreign, identified - stood at a peak from which it has ever since been falling. With that glory and with that prestige the public schools were closely linked, not only at home but among England's friends, enemies and subjects abroad. Imperial sentiment and English patriotism were widespread in the 'Mother Country' and the Empire, and the public schools may reasonably be looked upon as the central temples of the faith.

'Public schools' in the English sense are a purely English invention - perhaps the only English invention of first-rate importance in the field of education - and they are English in the most exclusive sense. 'Public school' itself, in English usage, has a meaning opposed to its meaning anywhere else, including Scotland, for it does not indicate a school either publicly owned or freely open to the public. Many attempts have been made to export public schools and the results, some bizarre, have been set out by J. A. Mangan.[2] This kind of school, however, has flourished in numbers only in England. Indeed, it is not far from the truth, and it would have been even nearer the truth in 1914, to say that all the most important public schools in Great Britain - all those with an indisputable claim to the title, except for two or three in Scotland - stand within 150 miles of London. Most, including the most famous three - Eton, Harrow, Winchester - are much closer.

The influence of the Victorian public schools spread widely and deeply in English society, but the number of boys who went to them, in proportion to the population as a whole, was tiny. Precise figures are impossible to arrive at because the term 'public school' has never been amenable to precise definition. J. R. de S. Honey suggests that in the last twenty years of the nineteenth century there may have been sixty-four 'leading public schools' plus an indefinite number of schools, not greater than forty, which could make some claim to the title.[3] If we allow an average of 300 boys per school, Honey's estimate gives a figure of rather fewer than 20,000 boys in the whole group of schools - considerably fewer in the 'leading' schools - at any one time. 20,000 represents about 1 per cent of the number of boys between fifteen and nineteen years old recorded in Great Britain at the Census of 1901.[4] The number of men in the population with personal knowledge of public schools as boys, as masters, or as parents must always have been a fraction of the whole: tiny in numbers but of enormous influence.

The Victorian public schools fastened themselves into the mind of the mass of the nation far less through their existence in fact than through the stories told about them in fiction. No other kind of school has generated so much imaginative writing, mostly during the century or so following the publication, in 1857, of *Tom Brown's Schooldays,* which established the *genre.* Most of it was aimed at the same market as the market for boys' adventure stories, discussed in Chapter Two, and the output of successful authors was on the same scale of volume and frequency. 'Imaginative' is the right adjective in more ways than one. Some writers, including three of the best-known - Thomas Hughes (*Tom Brown's Schooldays*), F. W. Farrar (1831-1903) (*Eric, or Little by Little* and *St Winifred's, or The World of School*), Rudyard Kipling (*Stalkey and Co.*) - had experience of the kind of schools they were writing about. There were others, including Talbot Baines Reed (1852-93), who wrote the well-known *The Fifth Form at St Dominic's,* had not. They did not let that stop them, least of all 'Frank Richards' or 'Martin Clifford' (both C. H. St J. Hamilton, 1875-1961), whose outpourings about Greyfriars in *The Magnet* and about St Jim's in *The Gem* (it is curious how many public schools in fiction and how few in fact have vaguely ecclesiastical names) began in 1908 and went on, week after week, until 1939 (*Gem*) and 1940 (*Magnet*). These stories must have given hundreds of thousands of boys a highly fantasised vision of life in schools which they would never enter. In one young mind at least they implanted the notion that, since school in fact did not seem like school in fiction, then the fact must be wrong.[5]

In another way, too, the influence of the public schools was brought to bear on thousands who never entered them. The Endowed Schools Acts of 1869 and 1874 encouraged the reform of ancient grammar schools, and by 1894, 1902 had been dealt with.[6] The obvious model for the reformers, freely used, was the public schools. They were the model, too, for county secondary schools set up under the Education Act 1902, and with a touch of irony, no doubt unconscious, for the organisation of the Borstal system for dealing with young criminals when it was founded between 1902 and 1908. As late as 1944 - well beyond the period we are concerned with - the influence of the Victorian public schools, with their emphasis on classical education, was strong enough to ensure that schools for academically gifted children would be called grammar schools, 'grammar' in this context having originally been the grammar of the classical languages. Schools for less gifted pupils were called secondary *modern* schools. In the public schools of the late nineteenth century the 'Modern Side', regarded with scorn by classicists, was always in danger of becoming a dustbin for dunces.

The late Victorian public schools have been admired and derided, praised and blamed, in their own day and since, for fanatical devotion to team games and to the British Empire. A connection between the two has always beeen recognised. Both have been regarded as essential elements in the 'public-school spirit', contributing to it a warlike tendency which to many people was far from unwelcome in the pre-1914 atmosphere: indeed, it was admirable.

This was a recent development. The Victorian public schools were in many ways an embodiment of instant tradition, very recently created, and some 'traditions' which late Victorians pointed to with pride and veneration would have surprised and probably pained Thomas Arnold and his generation of reformers. The ideal product of their sixth form, after education at Oxford or Cambridge, was a classical scholar in holy orders, not an Indian civil servant or an army officer, and while they had a due regard for 'manly exercises' as character builders they were aware that exaggerated love of games would be the enemy of the 'godliness and good learning' which they sought to instil.[7] In their scheme of things patriotism had a part, but not the imperialist patriotism of the 1880's and later. Military enthusiasm, by the eighties conspicuous, had no part in it at all.

It is not fanciful to trace the rise of the new spirit, in part, to the system of competitive entry into the public service which began with the first competition for places in the Indian Civil Service (ICS) in 1855, and was virtually completed some twenty years later after the ending of the purchase of commissions in the army. This system, which replaced patronage, was largely created by men of the class who increasingly sent their sons to the public schools, especially the new ones. Most of these boys had to find careers, preferably with good pay, security and high social standing - all of which could be found, in varying measure, in governing the Empire or in officering the army.

The ICS offered all three *desiderata* : high pay, security of tenure, high social standing, and on top of all a low retirement age (for those who lived to reach it) and a pension of £1,000 a year for life. Army officers had security (apart from certain occupational hazards) and high social standing but pay, except in the engineers and artillery, was scarcely enough to live on and in 'good' - that is, aristocratic - regiments, especially the Guards and cavalry, it was taken for granted that officers would have private money. On the other hand, all officers took rank socially as gentlemen, even sappers and gunners, and the general conditions of life offered horses, good fellowship, sport. The Indian Army, which British regiments regarded with condescension, was better paid, rank for rank, than the British service and offered a high standard of living relatively cheaply: it attracted boys (or their parents) for whom a military career might otherwise have been too expensive, and also those who had a family tradition of Indian service. Naval officers hardly entered into this scheme of things because by tradition they went into the service too young to have been to a public school.

It is not surprising, therefore, that the clients of the public schools should have turned their attention increasingly towards India and the army, British or Indian according to circumstances. The openings, running perhaps at thirty or forty a year for the ICS and a couple of hundred or so for the army, of which a minority would lead to the Indian Army, were numerous enough to encourage hope but competition, especially for the ICS., entered through the universities, was brisk. Those who succeeded, those who hoped to succeed, and all those associated with them - schoolmasters, relations, friends, dependants - combined to idealize and glamourise the institutions on which their hopes were set.

At the same time as imperial and military enthusiasm was mounting, but for different reasons, the cult of games was taking hold, culminating in that contradiction in terms, 'compulsory games'. The mania would have displeased headmasters of an earlier generation and it did not go uncriticised in its own day. It has been extensively studied, most recently by J. A. Mangan. Easy generalisations about its origins, he points out, are to be avoided, but it seems to have arisen partly amongst the boys and partly, perhaps mainly, among headmasters determined to get unruly pupils under control and to civilise their alcoholic, violent and often lawless amusements, which included poaching. Games were no doubt preferable, but at Rugby boys are said at one time to have worn football boots tipped with iron 'which much resembled the ram of an ironclad.' G. E. L. Cotton (1813-66), taking over in 1852, the [head]mastership of Marlborough, which had a particularly lurid reputation for mutiny and riot, deliberately set out to cultivate games and to appoint staff who could direct and take part in them. Cotton was a close friend of C. J. Vaughan (1816-97), Headmaster of Harrow from 1844 to 1859, another who was early in recognising 'the possibilities in games for expending boys' energies and keeping them within bounds', but he relied more on the monitors than on the masters for persuading boys on to the playing fields.'[8]

Other headmasters, including Dr J. J. Hornby (1826-1909) and Dr Edmond Warre (1837-1920) successively headmasters of Eton from 1868-1905, took a similar line. Like other admired features of public-school tradition, including prefects (monitors), fagging and 'houses', the passion for games seems to have emerged from policies developed by headmasters

[87]

(or forced upon them) to meet the necessities of their situation and to have been exalted later into matters of high moral principle and far-seeing wisdom. By 1893 E. M. Oakley, a public-school master, could observe: 'it is almost unnecessary to remark that the system of compulsory games is in full swing at Clifton, to the enormous benefit of all ...'[9]

Imperial and military enthusiasm in the late Victorian public schools, and enthusiasm for games, thus had a foundation in practicalities: the one in the necessity of finding a career or earning a living (often but not necessarily amalgamated), the other in the necessity of keeping boys in order by canalising their aggressive instincts. Round these hard cores rich clouds of sentiment quickly gathered, forming potent ingredients in that irrational *mystique* so abundantly generated by the public schools. Without something of the sort no institution is likely to have much power to command devotion. With it, extraordinary things are possible, as the outbreak of the Great War was to show.

On the practical side, pressure from parents obliged headmasters, often unwillingly, to adulterate classical education with forms of instruction more closely related to the demands of the late nineteenth century. Prominent among them were the demands, particularly for mathematics, of the examiners who kept the gates into the army through the Royal Military Academy at Woolwich, for the Royal Engineers and Royal Artillery, and, after 1870, the Royal Military College for infantry and cavalry at Sandhurst. In the early 1860's, when the Clarendon Commission investigated the public schools, the headmasters of the 'great schools' felt secure enough to suggest, with scarcely concealed contempt, that if that sort of thing was what parents really wanted for their sons, then the boys could get it from 'crammers' after they left school, and the cramming industry flourished down to 1914 and beyond.

The headmasters of the newer schools were in no position to be so haughty. The very existence of some of these schools including, at one time, Marlbough, founded in 1843, was downright precarious and some, such as Somerset College at Bath, collapsed. Survival depended on discreet observance of the maxim 'the customer is always right'. Therefore it was at the newer schools that the Modern Side first became established. The Clarendon Commissioners investigated it as something of a curiosity at Marlborough, Wellington (1856) and Cheltenham (1841). Clifton also had a Military Side,[10] and it was at these schools especially, though not solely, that the 'army class' or its equivalent became a standard feature.

So also in many schools, after the revival of the Volunteers in 1859, did the Cadet Corps or the Rifle Corps. Units were set up in the early 1860's at Marlborough, at Cheltenham, at Harrow and elsewhere, and by the 1880's they were widespread and some were specialised. To help boys aiming at Woolwich an Engineer Cadet Corps was founded at Clifton in 1875, and about 1890, with the same aim in view, the Rifle Corps at Cheltenham also became Engineers. Rifle shooting and military efficiency took their place among the activities in which public schools competed against each other, and in *Great Public Schools,* a highly laudatory volume published in 1893, the authors of the articles on the various schools, all themselves public school masters or ex-public schoolboys, usually include the Rifle Corps or the Engineering Corps under the heading of 'Games'. Cadets paraded before Queen Victoria during the Jubilee celebrations in 1897. King George V reviewed 17,000 in Windsor Great Park in 1911. By then the various schools' units had been reconstituted, as part of Haldane's reforms, as the Officers' Training Corps, which had senior units in the universities. By 1914 about 20,000 schoolboys and 5,000 undergraduates were enrolled in the appropriate branches of the OTC.[11]

Service as an army officer, especially in the Foot Guards, the cavalry and a few line regiments such as the 60th Rifles, was traditionally an aristocratic occupation, but aristocrats did not as a rule demean themselves to making it a profession, especially in the cavalry, where an officer attempting to enter the Staff College might be heavily discouraged. In no officers' mess was it considered 'good form' to discuss professional topics - 'shop' - and that tradition survived, somewhat attenuated, until the second World War. A large proportion of the boys leaving aristocratic schools, especially Eton, therefore became army officers for a few years, which might include a colonial campaign or two, before they devoted themselves to other aristocratic occupations such as politics, hunting, or local government and the management of the family estates.

As the army tradition spread to the middle-class schools of Victorian foundation, it took on a much more professional tinge, which it always had for the numerous officers recruited from the relatively impoverished Irish gentry. Wellington College, named after the Duke, not situated near Wellington, was founded mainly for the benefit of army families of limited means, whose sons would be likely to take soldiering seriously. In 1893 Cheltenham, fifty-two years after its foundation, was described as having 'Military rather than University aims.' The Revd T. A. Southwood, Head for many years of the Modern Side, was largely credited with 'the great success of Cheltenham as a military school', having taught many of the 1,700 Cheltonians who in the school's first fifty years went into the army. Clifton, founded in 1862, sent 500 boys into the army in its first thirty years, including Douglas Haig (1861-1928), the British Commander-in-Chief in France from 1915 to 1918.[12]

Not all public schools concentrated so heavily on getting boys into the army as Wellington, Cheltenham and Clifton, but most served to some extent as military academies and from the 1850's onward many began to glory in the fact by putting up war memorials. Outside Westminster School a pillar carries ten names from the Crimea and nine from the Indian Mutiny, including Commanders-in-Chief from both. For Winchester College William Butterfield (1814-1900) designed a Crimean memorial carrying thirteen names. By 1893 there were tablets on either side of the altar in the chapel of Cheltenham College carrying about seventy names: eleven killed in the Crimea, nineteen in the Mutiny, sixteen in the Second Afghan War, thirteen in Zululand and Egypt, 'and the rest in smaller wars in China, India, Ashanti and Burma.'[13] Campaigns on the Indian frontier in 1895 and 1897, in the Sudan in 1898, in South Africa from 1899 to 1902, and many that were more obscure added their complement of names to the schools' lists, foreshadowing plentifully by 1914 the far more crowded tablets soon to come.

Of twenty-two army officers who died between 1951 and 1960, distinguished enough to gain entry into the *Dictionary of National Biography,* eighteen went to schools listed by Honey among his sixty-four 'leading schools'. This is suggestive statistical evidence for the importance of public schools as recruiting centres for the army. Figures assembled for a study of the part played by public-school men in the Boer War are conclusive.[14] The author of the study, A. H. H. Maclean, defined sixty-two schools as 'public schools' on the basis of having provided at least fourteen officers each for service in South Africa. Of all regular officers who served in South Africa, he calculated that these sixty-two schools supplied nearly two-thirds - 5,669 (61.75 per cent) out of 9,180.

At the head of his list Maclean placed ten 'great public schools' - Eton, Harrow, Wellington, Cheltenham, Marlborough, Charterhouse, Clifton, Haileybury, Winchester, Rugby - which between them supplied 3,741 officers, 40.75 per cent of the total. Eton alone supplied 1,003, representing rather more than 28 per cent of all boys who left Eton between 1880 and 1900. From the ten 'great schools', some 13 per cent of all who left during that period served as regular officers in South Africa. From other schools, generally speaking, the proportion declines with declining prestige, though with some exceptions such as Kipling's old school, Imperial Service College at Westward Ho!

Thus at the turn of the century the army was taking a considerable proportion of the boys who went to the 'best schools', and generally speaking the 'better' the school the more of its boys the army took. From Eton, allowing for the fact that the figures relate only to the Boer War and the twenty years immediately before it, the true proportion might have been a majority. Maclean thought it would have been. In any case, the number of public school men who went into the army was large enough to ensure that the majority of army officers came from public schools and set the tone of army life. From the public-school boy's point of view, the demand for army officers was strong enough to ensure a strong tradition of military service in the schools, especially in the especially influential schools at the top of the tree.

The schools' other traditions might have been purposely designed, though there is no evidence that they were, to buttress the tradition of army service. Conditions of life were barrack-hard: no egalitarian critic of the public schools can justly acuse them of giving their privilieged pupils an easy life. A. G. Bradley (1850-1943), educated at Marlborough and the son of one of its early headmasters, says of his old school in its early days: 'might alone was right. Fighting was continuous and fierce. ... The place was not wholly bad. There was a freshness and manliness about it even then, and it is not perhaps surprising that this crude and turbulent period bred a great number of most admirable soldiers.' Marlborough's early traditions 'were Spartan in the extreme, and as such were taken pride in',[15] but no public school was comfortable. The buildings put up in the 19th century often had - and still have, if they have survived - an air of contrived bleakness or, in Sir Nicholas Pevsner's words, 'hearty and confident gloom'.

The boys, as prefects, were responsible for a good deal of the discipline of the school and in many schools were almost entirely responsible for running the games: responsibilities highly conducive, it was claimed, to the 'character-building' which was the main aim of public-school education. As Mangan points out, they had the enthusiastic support of the staff, especially of housemasters. As the games mania rose to its height in the twenty-five years or so before 1914 it was possible for a games-mad young man to move from school to Oxford or Cambridge, gather fresh athletic laurels and possibly a degree, and then spend the rest of his life as a games-playing schoolmaster.[16]

It was taken for granted that all boys, unless they were 'loafers' or 'swots', would be keen on games - 'the ideal of the average boy', wrote Leonard Huxley (1860-1933), an assistant master at Charterhouse, later editor of the *Cornhill Magazine,* 'is to be an athlete in some form or other, and satisfy that fine Teutonic craving for muscular expansion which fires the true Briton'[17] - and games focussed loyalties narrowly and intensely on the schools and on the houses within them: an excellent preparation for the inculcation, a little later, of loyalty to a regiment. Most of the qualities valued in the public schools, including the hearty, stoical behaviour needed for survival in such surroundings, with a carapace over the emotions, and a strong sense of duty, were serviceable in war. Beneath the carapace, emotional fires burned brightly. These austere schools generated in many boys a passionate, romantic, lifelong attachment to themselves and to their ideals which must surely be unique in the history of education. High among their ideals was patriotism.

II

Boys with artistic gifts were often unhappy in the confidently philistine atmosphere of Victorian public schools. Two eminent exceptions to this rule were the composer Sir Hubert Parry (1848-1918), an Etonian, and Sir Henry Newbolt the poet, who was at Clifton. Both were good at games and both, no doubt as a consequence, enjoyed school life.

Newbolt was among the public schools' most enthusiastic propagandists and if his predilection for poetry is overlooked he was as typical a late Victorian public-school man as it would be possible to find. He came of the class, the upper middle class, which provided many of their founders and supporters, being the son of a clergyman and the grandson of a naval officer. He was born in 1862, the year when Clifton College was founded, and he went there as a day-boy in the first flush of its success under Dr John Percival (1834-1918), whom he greatly admired. He may have heard the sermon Percival preached before leaving, in 1879, to become President of Trinity College Oxford:

> To-day we may say without fear of contradiction (and why should the false pride that apes humility prevent us from saying it, and drawing our lessons from it?), that there are few schools more widely or more favourably known throughout our kingdom and its dependencies; that there are few, if any, that possess a fuller, more varied, a more active, and, let us thank God for it, a purer life.[18]

Newbolt, who besides being good at games was an accomplished classical scholar, enjoyed what Clifton gave. No wonder he praised the system in which Clifton shone.

Newbolt, though never a soldier himself, took pains to emphasise the military associations of the public schools and to link them with the cult of games. In *The Book of the Happy Warrior,* a curious work of perverse scholarship published in 1917 but drawing on earlier writings, he went so far as to trace the origins of public schools to the medieval custom of sending boys of good family away from home to learn proper behaviour and all necessary accomplishments in great households:

The old method of training the young squires to knighthood produced our public school system, which is not at all the same as the monastic system. The monastic kind of school aimed at making clerics or learned men, and it was as much like a juvenile monastery as possible. The public school, on the other hand, has derived the housemaster from the knight to whose castle boys were sent as pages; fagging, from the services of all kinds which they there performed; prefects, from the senior squires, or "masters of the henchmen"; athletics, from the habit of out-of-door life; and the love of games, the "sporting" or "amateur" view of them, from tournaments and the chivalric rules of war.[19]

This audacious theory enabled Newbolt, by historical sleight of hand, to derive the Victorian public schools from an idealised version of the medieval institution of chivalry - 'a plan of life', he called it, 'a conscious ideal, an ardent attempt to save Europe from barbarism, even when nations were at war with each other.' Arnold of Rugby referred, less romantically, to 'all the curses of the age of chivalry', but at Clifton under Percival, says Mark Girouard, 'chivalry played an important part in its code.'[20]

Up-dating chivalry was a favourite nineteenth-century game, running at least as far back as the Eglinton Tournament of 1839, and there were many players, including those who spent their formative years in public schools. 'The chivalrous gentleman of Victorian and Edwardian days', says Mark Girouard, '... can be watched at work from the public schools to the Boy Scouts, and from Toynbee Hall to the outposts of the British Empire.'[21] Kipling made Norman knights express Victorian notions of chivalrous behaviour.[22] Baden-Powell, following a train of unhistorical thought similar to Newbolt's and just as baseless, attributed the origins of Boy Scouts to chivalry. 'The knights of old', he said, 'were the patrol leaders of the nation, and the men-at-arms were the Scouts ... the knight would daily ride about looking for a chance of doing a good turn to any needing help, especially a woman or child ... in distress'; and he cited a Knight's Code, including the precept 'Maintain the honour of your country with your life', as 'the first rules ... from which the Scout Law of today comes.'[23] Fantasy of this kind, harmless, even beneficent, in peacetime, was all too likely to to play a part, whether in the public schools or among the Boy Scouts, in building up a notion of the nature of war totally false and hopelessly romanticised.

Chivalry, for Newbolt, had the further advantage that it could be made to supply an ancient and distinguished pedigree for organised games. Apart from the passage already quoted from *The Happy Warrior*, Newbolt wrote a story called 'France *v* Gentlemen of England', dealing with the Jousts of St Inglebert held near Calais in March 1390. He calls the event 'the greatest and most typical athletic meeting of the Middle Ages' and has one of his characters saying 'We are in strict training.'[24]Sport, for Newbolt as for many others, is the peace-time face of war. 'If our games are to be a thorough training for war',he wrote in 1917, 'they must include throwing the bomb as well as the cricket ball, racing not only in boats, but in aeroplanes and armoured cars.[25] This alarming suggestion followed a line of thought that Newbolt had been expressing for years, usually in verse, and especially in thirteen pieces, collected at the request of the headmaster of Clifton College, which appeared under the title *Clifton Chapel and Other School Poems*. They included two of the best-known of Newbolt's poems: 'Clifton Chapel' and 'Vitäi Lampada'. These poems between them present a view of the interrelationship between school life, organised games, war and Christianity which, to judge from their innumerable re-printings, awoke widespread enthusiasm.

The public schools were nearly all Anglican institutions. Their headmasters, nearly all clergymen, liked to claim that school life centred on the chapel. Perhaps, but 'Clifton Chapel', written in 1898, suggests a special brand of Anglicanism with little of the New Testament in it and a good deal of the fiercer juices of the Old, together with a strong infusion of the more austere elements of classical paganism. Percival, according to Newbolt, claimed to follow 'the tradition of Arnold of Rugby' which 'derived originally from the patriotism or public spirit of the Jew, the Greek and the Roman. No other influence, he [Percival] would say, has produced so great a growth of the sterner and more robust virtues - fortitude, self-reliance, intrepidity: devotion to the common weal: readiness for united action and self-sacrifice.'[26]

These are all military virtues. Honey has suggested that two themes emphasised in Victorian classical teaching were blind patriotism and the glorification of death in battle.[27] In the early 1860's at Rugby, taking an average through the school, boys spent seventeen hours out of twenty-two on the classics, leaving three for mathematics and two either for modern languages or 'natural philosophy' - that is, chemistry and electricity.[28] There is no reason to think that concentration on the classics at Rugby was unusually intense, and Rugby was exceptionally advanced in the teaching of science. Thirty or forty years on, the river of classicism running through the public schools had been considerably diluted from the 'modern side', but it was still the foundation of public-school education, especially for the brighter boys. It is impossible to over-estimate the impression which classical teaching made, generation after generation, even on the most unreceptive minds, and since Caesar's *Gallic Wars* and Tacitus's *Agricola* were two of the easier Latin texts the military flavour of Roman culture must have been apparent even to the least talented students of ancient literature.

'Clifton Chapel' certainly displays mingled biblical and pagan influences. The god worshipped in the chapel is evidently that tribal deity the Lord of Hosts

> Who built the world of strife,
> Who gave his children Pain for friend
> And Death for surest hope of life.

The poet's son, to whom the poem is addressed, is expected to take 'vows of war' and 'to count the life of battle good And dear the land that gave you birth.' As soon as the oath has been taken

> To-day and here the fight's begun,
> Of the great fellowship you're free;
> Henceforth the School and you are one,
> And what you are, the race shall be.

In the last, most famous, verse the classical inspiration is obvious. The boy's attention is drawn to a memorial to an officer killed in some far-off imperial skirmish:

> God send you fortune, yet be sure,
> Among the lights that gleam and pass,
> You'll live to follow none more pure
> Than that which glows on yonder brass:
> "*Qui procul hinc*", the legend's writ -
> The frontier grave is far away -
> "*Qui ante diem periit,*
> *Sed miles, sed pro patria.*"

With 'Vitäi Lampada' Newbolt moves from the chapel to another sacred site: the cricket field - 'There's a breathless hush in the Close to-night.' Round cricket all the mythology and mysticism of the Victorian cult of team games gathered with peculiar intensity. Cricket was the *English* national game, scarcely understood elsewhere in the British Isles, but played with enthusiasm in the colonies and by some of the black and brown subject races of the Empire. It was called 'the greatest of school games' by a writer on Cheltenham College in 1893.[29] It was played by gentlemen who were amateurs and sportsmen. Into those words much of the essence of the public-school spirit could be distilled.

The extreme importance attached to the standing of a gentleman, traditional in English society before 1914 and reinforced by the nineteenth-century revival of chivalry, is becoming difficult to grasp, so greatly have values and attitudes changed over a period of seventy or eighty years. To be accepted as a gentleman was far more important than having a title, and titles, though coveted by some county families, were refused by others. A gentleman's rank carried impeccable social standing and conferred natural authority which a gentleman's inferiors were expected to accept, as, in traditional society, they were generally willing to do.

A gentleman was expected to observe exacting standards of personal conduct, particularly in matters of truth, honesty, and the performance of duty. There is little doubt that the Victorians expected more of a gentleman in these matters than had been expected in earlier times, partly, no doubt, through the influence of evengelical Christianity and partly, perhaps, because so many more men had the means to aspire to gentility. On the fringes of the cult of the gentleman there was snobbery and absurdity, particularly in conventions of dress, speech and manners, but the high standards aimed at were taken seriously, and against those who fell short of them their social equals brought uncompromising sanctions into play.

A gentleman's part in society was to provide leadership, to command and to govern. Games he played because he enjoyed them. On no account would he play games for money. He was an amateur, a status he greatly valued, and in games the word 'professional', like the term 'tradesmen' in good society, was a term of disdain. Nevertheless gentlemen would pay professionals to make up a team, especially at cricket, and to teach their sons games at public schools. The captain of any cricket team in which gentlemen played would of course be a gentleman and an amateur, and the tradition did not die out until after the second World War. From the assumption that captains of cricket teams would always be gentlemen it was a short step, readily taken, to the assumption that public-school boys would be the officers of Kitchener's armies.

A gentleman, on and off the playing fields, was at all times a 'sportsman'. It can hardly be accidental that the word took on its peculiarly English overtones at the time when the public schools were at the height of their influence, and the *Shorter Oxford English Dictionary'* dates the definition 'one who displays the typical good qualities of a sportsman' to 1894. Earlier in the century the term would have been associated with the ancient field sports of the gentry, but in its application to team games 'sportsmanship' was a quality in which Englishmen generally and public-school men particularly took great pride. It was one of the things that distinguished the English from 'lesser breeds without the law'. In 1915 Sir Arthur Conan Doyle (of Irish extraction) compared the 'military spirit' of the Germans unfavourably with the 'sporting spirit', believing 'that it was England's invention, and the chief characteristic of Englishmen.' [30] Anyone who wanted to accuse an Englishman of unsporting behaviour could not do it more plainly than by saying 'That's not cricket'.

Conversley, almost any kind of praiseworthy behaviour could be atttributed to the influence of cricket. In 'Vitäi Lampada', evidently much to the satisfaction of his public, Newbolt chose to indicate that cricket at Clifton could develop military qualities highly desirable in the Sudan. In the Close a magic formula is used to encourage a tail-end batsman:

...his Captain's hand on his shoulder smote -
Play up! Play up! and play the game!

In the Sudan the same tail-end batsman uses the same formula to encourage his troops in 'the wreck of a square that broke':

... the voice of a schoolboy rallies the ranks:
"Play up! Play up! and play the game!"

One poem might be dismissed as one poet's fantasy. Newbolt, however, was giving poetic, or at any rate metrical, expression to a belief held fervently in the public schools: that character-building was far more important than intellectual training and that in building character team games had a sovereign, almost mystical virtue. Dr J. E. C. Welldon (1854-1937), Bishop of Calcutta, an Etonian of high academic attainments and massive physique who had been headmaster successively at Dulwich College and at Harrow School, explained the doctrine to a Japanese audience in 1906, laying stress on its military and imperial implications:

'... I think, that in the training of an English gentleman, the games are more important than the studies. You will understand that I speak of the games, not as physical exercises, but as moral disciplines. ... The spirit of subordination and co-operation, the complete authority, the ready obedience, the self-respect and self-sacrifice of the playing-field enter largely into life. ... There is no cricketer worthy of the name ... who would not be glad to sacrifice himself if he could so win the victory for his side. Nay, the true sportsman, the true gentleman, will be careful, at whatever cost, to let others have the credit rather than himself. He will, if need be, take the second place, as that noble English soldier, Sir James Outram, did in the Indian Mutiny, when he generously surrendered to his junior officer, Sir Henry Havelock, the honour of relieving Lucknow, and he himself served in a civil capacity under him.
All these are qualities ... tending to produce what I may perhaps claim as a characteristic of the British race - the power of government; for it is a quality which the race has exhibited in relation to subject peoples at many periods of

English history in the many regions of the world where the flag of England flies.[31]

Rudyard Kipling, though he condemned team games as a frivolous distraction from the serious business of preparing for war (p. 80 above), emphasized the military and imperial mission of the public schools as forcibly as Newbolt. He went to what might by courtesy be called a public school, but it was a cheap and minor one, whereas Newbolt's school was major and expensive. United Services College was founded at Westward Ho! in 1874, four years before Kipling went there, on principles of the utmost frugality, by a group of retired army officers, none well-off, who wished to get their sons into Woolwich or Sandhurst as cheaply as possible. They put in as headmaster Cormell Price, who had shown a talent at Haileybury for getting boys through exams in modern-side subjects.[32]

In the row of boarding-houses in which the school was established the stony practicalities which underlay all public-school life showed through more prominently than in Clifton Chapel. Perhaps that was why Kipling, in 'The Flag of their Country', asserted the dislike and embarrassment of deeply patriotic schoolboys for a display of over-blatant patriotism. Perhaps, too, it was why, when Kipling considered the purpose of the school, he was even more single-minded than Newbolt, for USC had to be even more single-mindedly military than Clifton:

> With the last week of the term the Old Boys began to arrive, and their welcome was nicely proportioned to their worth. ... Recreants who, failing for the Army, had gone into business or banks were received for old sake's sake, but in no way made much of. But when the real subalterns, officers and gentlemen full-blown ... came on the scene ... the school divided right and left in admiring silence.[33]

USC sent 103 regular officers to the Boer War, 85 fewer than Rugby but 63 more than Westminster.[34]

'Practically the whole governing class of Englishmen', Bishop Welldon told his Japanese audience, in which was the Minister of Education, 'is educated in the public schools.'[35] Probably this was true. The schools were at the height of their prestige, and although it was possible to reach the governing heights without going to one - Lloyd George, Milner, Northcliffe, W. H. Lever come to mind, as also the fact that the two of them who had sons (Lloyd George and Lever) sent them to public schools - yet a public school was the recognised place of education for anyone who had been born a gentleman or whose parents wished him to be accepted as one. Moereover in the sixty years or so before 1906 the number of public schools, major and minor, had grown so rapidly that more boys than ever before had gone to one.

Welldon explained the nature of the public schools' influence, relying chiefly on his experience as a boy at Eton in the early 1870's and as headmaster of Harrow from 1885 to 1898. For Eton and Harrow he claimed: 'no other schools have done more, or perhaps so much, for the formation of the character exhibited now for several centuries by the statesmen, administrators, and reformers, the men of action and, although in less degree the men of thought, who have created or dignified the Empire.' The claim, no doubt made in good faith, was fraudulent. It exhibited the widespread habit, noticeable in the works of Kipling and Newbolt, of projecting late Victorian notions of the public schools and the Empire backward towards times when neither the public schools nor the Empire existed in anything like their late Victorian form, so that the weight of immemorial tradition seemed to be discernible behind quite new institutions.

The most important function of the public schools, in Welldon's view, was the formation of the character of English gentlemen. Their principal occupation, for which the monitorial system prepared them, was 'the honourable exercise of the governing function in mankind.' He made it clear that to his mind 'the governing function' included military command.

In forming character, he said, the influence of the boys on one another - the 'public opinion' of the school - was probably more important than the influence of the masters. 'The rules which boys make for each other,' he observed, 'are often more stringent than any which masters make for them.' Lees Knowles MP (1857-1928), writing of Rugby in the early 1870's, says: 'we had a school heraldry with its rules so precise and so complete' that it was possible, with a knowledge of it, to assign to each boy in the school 'his house, his rank, and his dignity. ... But recently, I am sorry to say, our school heraldry has ... attracted the attention of the authorities, and it has been much altered or suppressed.'[36]

Welldon remarked on truthfulness ('an English gentleman will not tell a lie') and on courage. Then he came to his central point: the sense of honour. 'A man's sense of honour, the consciousness of his obligation to do all and more than all that can rightly be expected of him ... is the distinguishing mark of a gentleman. To violate it is, in common parlance, "bad form".' The thrust of his address was towards service to the Empire.

One who has received the education of an English gentleman will not wholly fail, however tight the place may be in which he finds himself. ... When he is put down in the face of duty ... he will know what to do, and he will do it. It is this reserve power lying hidden in the British race which is, I think, the hope of the Empire.

It was also to be an extremely strong driving force behind the response to the appeal for men in 1914.

The late Victorian public schools inspired intense and lifelong loyalty: in retrospect, perhaps the most remarkable thing about them. Welldon took it very seriously:

> The thought of the school becomes an inspiring motive in life. As the descendant of a noble family, so the member of a famous school is lifted above himself by his inherited associations. He shrinks from all that is lowering, he aspires to all that is honest and of good report, for the sake of the school which he loves.

Carrying matters further still, he quoted the example of 'the young Etonian soldier at Laing's Nek in Natal' who 'breathing the prayer *Floreat Etona* ... laid down his life.'

Did Welldon, an ex-headmaster, exaggerate the hold of the public schools on their old boys? Probably not greatly, for they were educational engines of enormous power, not yet under serious attack, operating not only directly but, much more widely, indirectly. They generated great pressure behind ideals and values, quintessentially English, which had a military element in them but were not for professional soldiers only. In 1914 all public-school men and that far larger number who accepted the things the public schools stood for knew that they were expected to abide by the same exacting code of conduct, the same exacting rules of 'good form', and that they would not be pardoned, by themselves as much as by others, if they failed. 'Non compliance with this demand', wrote the soldier-poet C. H. Sorley, born in 1895, educated at Marlborough, killed in 1915, 'would have made life intolerable.'[37] The outbreak of war took them by surprise, but there had been many years of psychological preparation. Donald Hankey, a Rugbeian killed on the Somme, summarized the public-school man's position: 'His whole training, the traditions of his kind, had prepared him for that hour. From his earliest school days he had been taught that it was the mark of a gentleman to welcome danger, and to regard the risk of death as the most piquant sauce to life.'[38]

CHAPTER SIX

Voluntary enlistment 1914-15: 'Your country needs YOU!'

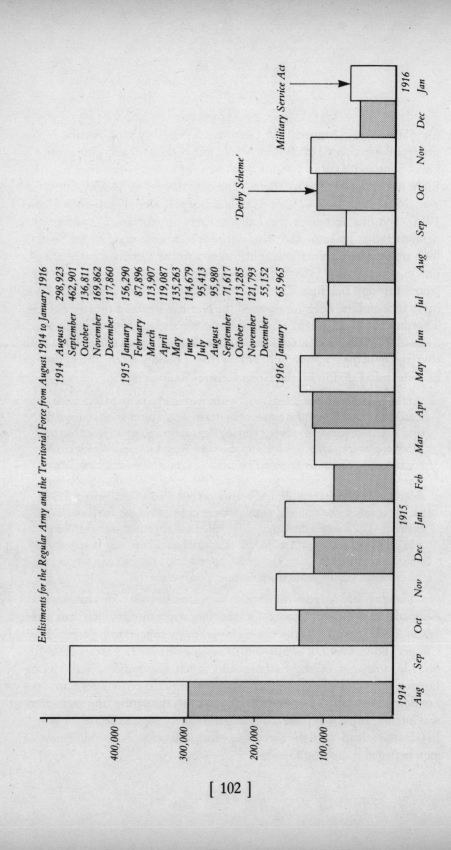

Enlistments for the Regular Army and the Territorial Force from August 1914 to January 1916

1914	August	298,923
	September	462,901
	October	136,811
	November	169,862
	December	117,860
1915	January	156,290
	February	87,896
	March	113,907
	April	119,087
	May	135,263
	June	114,679
	July	95,413
	August	95,980
	September	71,617
	October	113,285
	November	121,793
	December	55,152
1916	January	65,965

'Derby Scheme'

Military Service Act

I

On Saturday 1st August 1914 Germany declared war on Russia. It was uncertain whether Great Britain would join in, and the recruiting office at Great Scotland Yard in London was open for normal peacetime business. Eight men joined the army there.[1] The next day being Sunday, the office was closed. Not far away, in Trafalgar Square, Keir Hardie MP (1856-1915), the first leader of the Labour Party in parliament, addressed a demonstration by some thousands of people against war. At the level of high policy the Cabinet was split,[2] although the Germans were already moving against the French and were demanding free passage for their troops through Belgium. On Monday 3rd August Germany declared war on France and the Belgians rejected the German demand for free passage. That day was August Bank Holiday, so the recruiting office was still closed.

E. C. Powell, a seventeen-year-old bank clerk, spent the holiday with two friends in the Chiltern hills, not far from London. At the end of the day he came into London on the Great Central Railway:

> 'At the terminus,' he recalled later, 'when we emerged into Marylebone Road, we found London in a state of hysteria. A vast procession jammed the road from side to side, everyone waving flags and singing patriotic songs. ... We were swept along ... bitten by the same mass hysteria. Westward we poured in a torrent of frenzied humanity ... on to Buckingham Palace, where the whole road in front of the palace was chock-a-block with shouting demonstrators. Police were powerless to control the flood as people climbed the railings; sentries were clapped on the back and even chaired. "The King! The King!" they yelled and chorused, and then broke into the National Anthem. After this pandemonium had lasted for a considerable time the king and queen appeared on the balcony waving to the crowd. Only then did the multitude slowly disperse.'[3]

On Tuesday 4th August the British Government sent an ultimatum to Germany demanding respect for Belgian neutrality, which had been repeatedly recognised by the Great Powers in the nineteenth century. E. R. Cooper, Town Clerk of Southwold in Suffolk since 1895, captain of the fire brigade, manager of the harbour and much else besides, was visiting London. He 'came slowly up Whitehall through the crowd' on a bus. 'All London was awaiting Germany's reply to our Ultimatum, the excitement was intense, and it was plain that a large Majority were in favour of War.'[4] In Great Scotland Yard the recruiting office was open. A 'seething mass' of men besieged it, hoping to enlist.[5]

Of the thousands whom young Powell heard shouting for the King on 3rd August, of the 'large Majority' who, Mr Cooper thought, were 'in favour of War' on 4th August, of the 'seething mass' at Great Scotland Yard recruiting office on the same day, it is a fair guess that few, if any, had had any thought of war until a few days earlier. Even in the Cabinet, we have it on Churchill's authority that the idea of war as a serious possibility did not present itself until Friday 24th July, when the terms of an ultimatum presented by Austria-Hungary to Serbia became known.[6] As late as 7th July, ten days after the murder at Serajevo which provoked the Austrian ultimatum, a meeting of German, British and American explosives makers who, of all men, might have been expected to be sensitive to rumours of war, were discussing the possibility of joining together in business in the United States.[7]

Civil war, breaking out in Ireland, seemed to the Cabinet until 24th July a much nearer and graver risk than war in Europe, and George Dangerfield has suggested that the tensions in British society, which had already shown themselves in a series of violent labour disputes since 1911, were mounting towards a general strike in the autumn of 1914 which might have carried violence to the point of revolution.[8] If these possibilities seem fantastical to a generation which has been brought up to regard the years before 1914 as a golden age, it is salutary to pay heed to Barbara Tuchman who 'can offer the reader a rule based on adequate research: all statements of how lovely it was in that era made by persons contemporary with it will be found to have been made after 1914', or to listen to Churchill: 'Was it astonishing that German agents reported and German statesmen believed that England was paralysed by faction and drifting into civil war, and need not be taken into account as a factor in the European situation?'[9]

The Germans may not have been so wrong as Churchill hints. Certainly it was the Germans' own policy which jolted the British into unity, for the Cabinet and the nation were far from unanimously in favour of war until the Germans attacked Belgium. All the evidence, including the reminiscenses of ex-soldiers, suggests that this was what struck the spark which set off the explosion of enthusiasm which visitors to London ran into on 3rd and 4th August 1914.

The suddenness of the onset of war fever and the way in which it smothered all other national preoccupations, greatly reducing the turbulence of home politics - even, for a time, of Irish politics - is one of the best-documented aspects of the outbreak of the Great War. Quarrels within the United Kingdom did not cease. Irish nationalism flared into the Easter Rising of 1916. Labour troubles rumbled on and then, between 1919 and 1921, erupted into what was perhaps a potentially revolutionary situation. Nevertheless early in August 1914 it was if a switch had been thrown, greatly reducing the pressure behind quarrels at home, greatly increasing it behind the quarrel with Germany, so that great reserves of bellicosity were concentrated behind the nation's military effort. The building up of this explosive concentration of warlike patriotism has been considered in earlier chapters. What was its practical effect on the raising of volunteer armies?

II

To raise these armies a miracle was required, and a war god was found to perform it: Lord Kitchener. To a generation which has been taught to have no heroes and which remembers him chiefly with a titter, from one over-parodied poster, Kitchener's pre-eminence during the first period of the Great War is almost impossible to comprehend. The imperial glory of his achievements in the Sudan, in South Africa, in India shone round him undimmed, so that in all matters to do with land warfare his omniscience, his infallibility, were taken for granted. More than that, his arrival near the head of affairs - he was taken into the Cabinet as Secretary of State for War on 5th August 1914-spread the same sort of general, indefinable confidence as that generated more than a quarter of a century later when Churchill bcame Prime Minister. Kitchener's death in HMS *Hampshire* on 5th June 1916, in stormy Northern seas, brought his career to an appropriately sombre and heroic end, with an atmosphere of Nordic doom about it, after his main work was done and before his reputation with the general public had suffered the eclipse which had already overtaken it in high places.

Clean against the accepted opinion of the day, even at the highest levels, Kitchener acted on the assumption that the war would last at least three years and that the Government would have to raise troops in continental numbers - the first time a British Government had ever done so. On 6th August Parliament sanctioned an extra half-million men for the army. On 7th a Press advertisement appeared:

YOUR KING AND COUNTRY NEED YOU
A CALL TO ARMS
An addition of 100,000 men to his Majesty's Regular Army is immediately necessary in the present grave National Emergency.
Lord Kitchener is confident that this appeal will be at once responded to by all those who have the safety of our Empire at heart.

TERMS OF SERVICE
General service for a period of 3 years or until the war is concluded. Age of enlistment between 19 and 30.[10]

In support of press advertising there very quickly appeared half a million copies of Army Form B218, a plain piece of black-and-white typesetting on a quarto sheet folded to give four pages of text. The front page, headed

YOUNG MEN, YOUR COUNTRY NEEDS YOU!

carried a message with Kitchener's facsimile signature. Its inelegant forcefulness strongly suggests that Kitchener drafted it himself:

> More men are urgently required for the Regular Army. They are required NOW. It is of no use sending untrained men into the field. If you want to help your country at this critical moment, you must come forward NOW, and be trained as a soldier.
>
> You will not be sent to the front until you are trained and fit to take the field against the enemy. As soon as you are trained you will be given the chance to show the stuff that is in you.
>
> You are not asked to join the Army in the ordinary way, which involves service in peace time, though you will be welcome if you do so. You are only asked to serve for the War. As soon as the War is over, every facility will be given you to secure your discharge, and get back to your ordinary work.[11]

The next page, headed 'What the Army will do for You', adds a seasoning of self-interest to the strong meat of patriotic duty: 'You are not asked to serve for the money you can make out of it, but to help your Country. At the same time it is worth mentioning what the conditions of service are.' Pay and allowances are quoted: 6s 8 $\frac{1}{2}$d (about 33p) a week for an infantry private, plus 1s 1d a week for his wife and 2d for each child. Medical requirements and other matters follow. The document ends, at Kitchener's personal insistence, it is said, with:

> God Save the King.

The advertisement and this pamphlet signalled the beginning of 'Kitchener's armies'. By the beginning of 1916, without the backing of legal compulsion, they numbered more than 1 $\frac{1}{2}$ million men. Nearly another three-quarters of a million - 725,842, according to official figures - came under arms, also without compulsion, by way of war-time enlistments in the Territorial Force.[12]

Against the Territorials, as part-time holiday amateurs, Kitchener had a rock-hard prejudice.[13] 'Keen and ardent youths', Churchill called them, 'of strong military predilections'[14], but in support of Kitchener it must be pointed out that in 1913 the number of 'ardent youths' in the Territorial Force was falling and fewer than 12 per cent of the officers and only 7.5 per cent of other ranks had volunteered for service overseas. By the time war broke out slightly under 7 per cent of all ranks had taken the Imperial

Service obligation, and there was no way in which those who had not taken it could be forced to do so.[15]

It is understandable that Kitchener preferred to raise forces on his own terms and under his own control, but it meant that Haldane's organisation, based on Territorial Associations in the counties and designed with wartime expansion in mind, was by-passed. Kitchener would not allow the Territorials to recruit above establishment until his first 100,000 men had come forward[16] and Haldane, aggrieved, complained in his autobiography:

> He [Kitchener] insisted on raising, not Territorial line after Territorial line, each of which would have stepped into the place of one in front as it moved away, but new "Kitchener" Armies through the medium of the Adjutant-General's Department of the War Office. The result was the confusion which arises from sudden departures from settled principles.[17]

Confusion there was - all contemporary records bear witness to it - but it is inconceivable that a system could have been designed which would not have broken down under the rush of volunteers in the first six or eight weeks of the war. By 25th August, only eighteen days after his first appeal, Kitchener could tell the House of Lords that his 100,000 recruits were 'already practically assured'. Three days later he called for 100,000 more, who came even faster. Four weeks after war broke out, 30,000 men attested in one day - about the number the War Office usually dealt with in a year - and in the fifth week 175,000 men joined Kitchener's army as well as an unrecorded number who became Territorials.

On 11th September the authorities, overwhelmed, raised the minimum acceptable height for infantrymen from 5 feet 3 inches to 5 feet 6 inches - a sidelong comment on the average height of working-class men before 1914 - but probably there was no need, for the tide was past its flood. Men never again came in so fast, whether volunteering or compelled. The voluntary system lasted from the outbreak of war until the end of 1915, fifteen months altogether, and of the 4,970,902 men who joined the British army during the war it raised almost exactly half: 2,466,719. Of the men raised in Great Britain in 1914-5 761,824 - 29 per cent - joined before the war was two months old. The number of recruits in September 1914 - 462,901 - was half as great again as the number in the month before, nearly three times as great as the greatest monthly total that followed (169,862 in November 1914) and almost five times the monthly average - 95,594 - during the fifty-two months of the whole war.[18]

These figures take no account of recruits from the Empire, since they are not directly the subject of this book, but enthusiasm in the white colonies, at the outset, ran high. 'Australians', says an Australian historian, '... were ready and indeed terrifyingly willing to go to war.' In Canada, during the course of the war, about 641,000 men were raised, in Australia, 417,000, in New Zealand 220,099, in South Africa 134,837, in other colonies, 135,000. The Indian Army raisd about 1.4m., but that was a different story.[19]

The 762,000 early volunteers in Great Britain, together with the quarter of a million men in the Territorial Force when war broke out, probably represented some 20 per cent of the men of prime military age - twenty to thirty-five years old - in the country. They must have needed little or no pressure to enlist, for there was scarcely time to bring pressure to bear before they made up their minds. Their motives are unlikely to have been purely patriotic. Young men would join the Territorials for companionship and an annual paid holiday. A good many, to judge from photographs of their dress and general appearance as they stood in queues outside recruiting offices, may have been escaping from back-street poverty, and certainly the recruiting posters made play with the pay, food and clothing which the army offered. Many joined because their friends did: it was 'the thing to do'. When all these motives are discounted, nevertheless, the fact remains that within two months of the outbreak of war about a million volunteers were under arms. This is striking testimony to the power of those influences which we have observed at work in the nation before 1914, instilling a particular conception of national and imperial greatness; cultivating certain standards of behaviour, notions of honour, ideas of patriotic duty; indicating with ever-increasing insistence whom the enemy would be.

Pressure in support of these influences began to be applied as soon as war broke out. It was channelled less through official bureaucracy than through the social structure and through voluntary organisations with a strong middle-class or upper-class tinge about them. Within three days of the outbreak of war the Government was appealing to lords lieutenant and the chairmen of Territorial Associations (often the same individuals) for help in raising Kitchener's army - not Territorials - and MP's quickly began recruiting on their own initiative. 'In one city of the Midlands', says Basil Williams, 'the local MP within 24 hours changed the recruiting office from a poky back street to the town hall, engaged eight civilian doctors to help the one overworked medical officer ... printed locally the sacred Army Forms for recruits with their seventeen elaborate questions, and had the bath ... cut out of the programme.'[20]

Nothing was more characteristic of the voluntary effort, in these earliest weeks of war, than the raising of 'pals' battalions'. Municipalities or private individuals were encouraged to advance money, later to be repaid, for clothing, feeding and housing battalions raised in their locality, which groups of 'pals' would join from motives of local as well as national patriotism. There was thus about the scheme an air of self-help and private munificence in keeping with the dominant liberal mentality of the day. At the same time, the proposal is said to have originated with the seventeenth Earl of Derby (1865-1948) - and others - so that it also had aristocratic associations equally gratifying to a society which 'loved a lord' and expected him to take a lead in voluntary public service.[21]

Ten battalions of infantry were raised in Newcastle-upon-Tyne, eight in Manchester, four in each of Glasgow, Salford and Hull. Lord Derby raised artillery for two divisions. His neighbour in north-west England, the second Duke of Westminster (1879-1953) raised an armoured-car section and took it on active service. In Newcastle-upon-Tyne Joseph Cowen and his sister provided £15,000 for equipping a Tyneside battalion.[22] Colonel E. C. Meysey-Thompson (1859-1944), a Unionist MP., and the London boroughs of Camberwell and Deptford each raised artillery for one division, and artillery of one kind or another was also raised by several other London boroughs, by Nottingham, by the West Yorkshire Coal Owners, by Colonel Hammersley.[23]

These locally-based recruiting schemes were highly successful.

The idea of men of the same town all serving together', wrote Basil Williams in 1918, 'caught hold of the people's imagination and aroused all that was best in local patriotism and emulation. The Mayor and Corporation generally constituted themselves recruiters ... and the inhabitants took a personal interest in the rapid raising and clothing of their own battalions, in the high standard of clothing and equipment of the men and their comfort during training. Local landowners lent their parks ... and business men lent their warehouses ... and spent much time and money in perfecting the organisation for the purchase of supplies or the erection of huts.[24]

The idea of local recruiting took hold particularly in large towns, no doubt because of the density of the population. As early as Friday 28th August 1914 Lord Derby, on his home ground in Liverpool, invited the clerks of that city to form a battalion. By Monday 31st they had formed two, by Tuesday they had completed a brigade by forming a third, and by the following Monday a fourth battalion was ready as the basis for another brigade. In three days 4,000 recruits came in. Pals' battalions were readily raisable even after the early head of steam had gone out of recruiting. On Tyneside between 23rd October and 1st November 1914 three battalions were sanctioned and by 18th November a fourth was complete: all at the same time as other battalions were being raised in the same district. Just before Christmas 1914 Sir William Lever (1851-1925), head of a very large group of soapmaking firms and other businesses, wrote to Jules Renkin, Minister for the Colonies in the Belgian Government-in-exile:

> I visited one of the Camps at Salisbury Plain yesterday where we have six hundred men from Port Sunlight [the site of Lever's main factory] with five hundred others from the same district, a total of eleven hundred men in one battalion. These form part of the million men for Lord Kitchener's Army, which are now preparing by drilling and training to take the field. All the men were full of keenness to get to the Front, and to avenge the wrongs done to Belgium.[25]

At Port Sunlight there is a very large war memorial with nearly 500 names.

Pals' battalions were not confined to the North. In London they were raised in Wandsworth, Lambeth and Camberwell - three - and no doubt elsewhere as well. Units were also raised, in London and elsewhere, which were composed of men of similar occupations or common interests. In November 1915 *The Times* reported a footballers' battalion, three battalions of sportsmen (23rd, 24th, 30th Royal Fusiliers, a London regiment), a company of boxers, a company from Fiji, a platoon of Rhodesians in the 6th King's Royal Rifles, socially a desirable regiment, and battalions for farmers, butchers, bankers and bantams (men between 5' 2" and 5' 4" tall). There were three bantams' battalions and in Wales a whole division was formed of men between 5' and 5' 3".[26] There were also public-schools' battalions, evidently based on a wide definition of 'public schools'. 118 Infantry Brigade - 5,000 men - consisted entirely of public-schools' battalions of the Royal Fusiliers.

The Legion of Frontiersmen and other organisations and individuals sought recruits motivated by the spirit associated with 'outposts of Empire'. An advertisement in the *Evening Standard* of 15th January 1915 addressed them:

> Frontiersmen - Thousand Wanted for Secret Mission. To serve under F. C. Selous, Lieut-Col D. P. Driscoll, Cherry Kearton &c. "It is a splendid opportunity", said Col. Driscoll, "for men with the old English spirit of enterprise. They will get all the fun and all the fighting they want." ... not a penny of the cost of raising the battalion will have fallen on the authorities.[27]

F. C. Selous (1851-1917), an old Rugbeian, was one of the founders of Rhodesia. When war broke out he was already over sixty and he had some difficulty in persuading the War Office to employ him, but he was eventually commissioned in the Royal Fusiliers. D. P. Driscoll (1862-1934), a leading figure in the Legion of Frontiersmen, was a regular officer who had served in Burma and South Africa. Cherry Kearton (1871-1940) was a well-known naturalist and explorer who gave his address, in *Who's Who,* as 'The Jungle, Kenley, Surrey'.[28] The unit which was the subject of the advertisement was the 25th Royal Fusiliers, which served under Col Driscoll against the Germans in East Africa. Selous won the DSO in 1916 and at the age of 66, in 1917, was killed in action.

Most of the units raised from 'pals' or on some similar basis were infantry battalions. Basil Williams traced 172. Of gunners he mentions 84 brigades, a brigade in the Royal Artillery (later known as a 'regiment') being in 1914-5 roughly the equivalent of an infantry battalion, and of Royal Engineers 48 companies. An entire division (38th), with reserves, was raised in Wales, and a brigade of 'bantams' as well.[29] What Williams omits to point out in his enthusiastic account of these units is that when a pals' battalion was caught in heavy fighting the effect in its locality was devastating as, for instance, when pals' battalions went into action on the Somme in 1916.

III

'The popular conception of "a rush to the colours", says Clive Hughes in an essay on 'The New Armies', 'is inaccurate.'[30] This judgment is suprising. What would have constituted a 'rush' if $2\frac{1}{2}$ million recruits in fifteen months did not? It is in line, however, with some contemporary comment. In 1916 a contributor to *The Times History of the War,* possibly H. W. Wilson (1866-1940), well-known in his day as a writer on military and naval matters, observed: 'A considerable, though not a very remarkable, increase of recruiting followed immediately on the Government's appeal .' Without pausing to explain what would have qualified as 'very remarkable' Wilson went on: 'The country was in no sense awake ... a frame of mind not easily to be moved, even by the advertising campaign ... set on foot by the Parliamentary Recruiting Committee, at the suggestion of the War Office, on August 31st.'[31]

The Parliamentary Recruiting Committee, the subject of an article by Roy Douglas in 1970,[32] held a preliminary meeting on 27th August 1914. It had been brought into existence, possibly with Asquith's encouragement but apparently without peace-time planning, to unite MP's of all parties behind the drive for recruits, and it evolved, says Cate Haste, out of the National Liberal Federation.[33] The party leaders were presidents and they were supported by an imposing, plentifully coronetted, array of all-party political talent and social glamour.[34]

At the first and only full meeting of the committee, on 31st August 1914, nine Liberal MP's were present, with two Unionists (Conservatives) and two from Labour. The War Office was represented by two staff officers.[35]

There were never at any time any Irish Nationalists on the Committee although some (see below) are said to have worked for it. It is a fair guess that the individual chiefly responsible for keeping the PRC going was its Clerk, R. H. Davies CB (1872-1970). He was Patronage Secretary to the Treasury and had formerly been Private Secretary to Viscount Gladstone (1854-1930), W. E. Gladstone's youngest son. He was later Secretary to the Central Liberal Association and he ended his career as Private Secretary to the Principal of the University College of North Wales at Bangor.[36] Perhaps he was one of those who, like Lord Hankey, delight in exercising power at one remove. He must have been a very hard worker, for the PRC was extremely active throughout the period of voluntary enlistment.

The Committee's purpose was to get the political parties to combine to use their organisation and their skill, chiefly in the constituencies, to bring men into the army. They could provide premises, staff, experienced speakers, skill in running meetings. Perhaps most important of all, they had a detailed knowledge of the population, built up from voters' lists for canvassing, such as no Government department could provide without a national register. Moreover they could and did build up their knowledge by an extension of canvassing techniques.

Asquith told Parliament that the PRC received 'a small sum' from the Government and *The Times* once described it as 'a sort of annexe to the War Office',[37] but it was essentially a very large creation of voluntary unpaid effort. In the words of Basil Williams in 1918:

Tories and Radicals, Labour members and Irishmen, hardly on speaking terms before the war, toured about the country together in caravans, or made lightning journeys from the Land's End to Sutherlandshire to meet on the same platforms or at the same street corners. ... The speakers were chiefly ... over military age, all, of course, unpaid. ... Sometimes, men wounded from the Front would speak. ... Other volunteers [worked in offices]. ... The motorists of the Kingdom, through their principal club, put their automobiles at the disposal of the War Office. ... The hoardings were covered with the posters issued by the Parliamentary Recruiting Committee.[38]

The PRC's organisation grew with the war. By the autumn of 1915 there was a local PRC in nearly every constituency, usually with the lord lieutenant, the mayor, or some other dignitary in the chair, working with the military authorities. In London, by this time, there were five departments: Householders' Return and Inquiries; Finance; Publications; Meetings; Publicity.

The Householders' Return and Inquiries Department ran a postal canvass, supervised by Davies and J. Malcolm Fraser, which anticipated the National Registration Act 1915 (p. 125 below) and must be one of the largest operations ever carried out by a voluntary organisation. Eight million letters were sent out, one to every householder on the electoral register in Great Britain, with a form on which each householder was asked to enter the name of any man under his roof who was willing to join the army for the duration of the war. As returns came in they were sorted by 2,000 volunteers, men and women, working from ten in the morning until ten at night. Even so, the job took several weeks. 'Good papers', containing the names of potential recruits, were sent to recruiting officers. 'The result of the householders' returns', said *The Times* rather cautiously, 'was to secure a very large number of recruits.' As a side effect, they also enabled wives, mothers and dependents to trace soldiers who had omitted to arrange the payment of separation allowances.[39]

Through its Publicity Department the PRC., in its life of about sixteen months, is said to have issued 54 *million* posters, leaflets and other publications, to have organised 12,000 meetings and to have arranged more than 20,000 speeches[40]: in all, an advertising campaign on a scale never previously approached and rarely, if ever, equalled or exceeded since. The Committee retained at least one advertising agency - Caxton[41] - but even for an experienced advertising man, and most of those connnected with the PRC were not advertisng men at all, the product was not easy to promote. Packaged though it might be in the trappings of patriotic duty, military glory, hearty good fellowship, manly adventure, it was in fact terror, wounds and death. After the first enthusiasm faded it became extremely hard to sell and eventually Major Gossett, one of the War Office's representatives, urged that meetings and publications should be 'damped down'.[42]

The feverish atmosphere of the times is transmitted through the great number of poster designs. The PRC issued about 150, many of them minor variations of each other, so that there were perhaps a hundred distinct subjects: a large number for a period of about a year and a quarter. With other bodies issuing posters at the same time, the total result, on poster-sites all over the country, must have made a formidable visual onslaught. The collection at the Imperial War Museum, representative but by no means complete, will support a few general remarks.[43]

Some posters relied on typeset or drawn lettering, but most carried illustrations, varying from a large and terrifying photograph of a beckoning sergeant to John Bull, irritable, over-weight and out-of-date as usual. Allegorical figures, as in the political cartoons of the time, were fairly frequent. In May 1915, when a German submarine commander sank the liner *Lusitania,* killing nearly 1,200 people, an angry lady appeared, walking on the waves in front of the sinking ship and calling for volunteers. Among the symbols of patriotism Boy Scouts sometimes figure, notably in a design by Baden-Powell himself, using his considerable artistic talent to show a chain of supply from a workshop to a gun *via* a woman factory worker, a nurse and a Boy Scout who is handing a packet of ammunition to a sailor standing near a field-gun served by a soldier. A gormless civilian, nattily dressed, looks on uncomprehending above the question 'Are YOU in this?' Soldiers generally appear either as cheerful devil-may-care 'pals' or as figures of ferocity, including a thoroughly anachronistic charging cavalryman. Realistic scenes of trench warfare are lacking, which is hardly to be wondered at, especially since few if any of those concerned with commissioning or designing the posters had first-hand knowledge of what they were encouraging men to volunteer for.

Most of the messages on the posters fall into a few well-defined categories. Many, especially early on, appealed simply to patriotism: 'Rally round the Flag', 'Fight for King and Empire', 'Lend your strong right arm to your country' and the tirelessly repeated 'Your Country needs YOU' and its variants. Some messages were topical - 'Remember Belgium!', 'Remember Scarborough!' (bombarded from the sea in the autumn of 1914), 'Remember the LUSITANIA!' - or emphasised German beastliness, such as one carrying Kitchener's assertion: 'The Germans act with the same barbarous savagery as the Sudan Dervishes.'

There are repeated variations on the theme 'Lads, you're wanted, GO and HELP' which shade off towards the large group of posters exerting some kind of moral blackmail. 'Why are *you* stopping HERE when your pals are out THERE?' says one, and another: 'You're proud of your pals in the Army, of course! But what will your pals think of YOU?' Some play on post-war shame: 'What will your answer be when your boy [shown in silhouette as a Boy Scout] asks you - "Father, what did *you* do to help when Britain fought for freedom in 1915?".'

The poster designers often addressed women, but they could never quite make up their minds whether to assume that women would take the line 'Women of Britain say - *"Go!"'* or whether to accuse them of holding their men back, as in 'Four Questions to the Women of Britain':

1. You have read what the Germans have done in Belgium. Have you thought what they would do if they invaded this country?
2. Do you realise that the safety of your home and children depends on our getting more men NOW?
3. Do you realise that the one word "GO" from you may send another man to fight for our King and Country?

4. When the War is over and some one asks your husband or your son what he did in the Great War, is he to hang his head because you would not let him go?

There seem to have been no posters, either among those issued by the PRC or produced by other bodies, which made any directly sexual approach. This is surprising, considering the age-old links between war and virility.

As well as posters the PRC, as Basil Williams indicates, produced a great deal of other printed matter. A catalogue issued in March 1915, of which 5,000 copies were printed, lists thirty-five pamphlets and leaflets - more were issued later - and offers to supply them in sets without charge. 'Quantities for distribution', it goes on, 'can also be supplied without charge, it being understood that the person making the request undertakes to see that the literature is carefully and effectively distributed. A series of POSTERS has also been issued, samples and particulars of which can be obtained.'[44]

The pamphlets and leaflets covered much the same ground as the posters. Nos 1, 1A and 1B, of which at least 5.8 million, probably more, were printed, gave terms of enlistment, pay and allowances. No 2 reproduced a cartoon by Bernard Partridge, typical of his work, showing Liberty comforting Belgium. No 3 carried a manifesto from members of the PRC to trade unionists. No 5 reported speeches made by the Prime Minister, Asquith, and other leading politicians - Bonar Law, Balfour, Churchill - at a recruiting meeting held at the Guildhall in London on 4th September 1914. Among the rest were a patriotic song sheet (No 11); appeals for more men (7, 16); more Partridge (18); a good deal of atrocity propaganda; 'Our Religious Leaders on a Just and Righteous War' (22); 'Three Questions to Employers'(30) and 'Our Village and the War' (33) by Mrs F. S. Boas, wife of a prolific scholar in English literature who eventually became Reader in Indian History at Oxford.[45] 'Why,' says Mrs Boas, 'won't any chap here in Little Bidworth [fictitious] fight another chap twice his size any day if he sees him doing a bit of bullying on a kid?'

Pamphlets and leaflets, like posters, were issued by many other bodies besides the PRC. One ingredient they had which the posters had not was verse. A small selection follows:[46]

ENGLAND WHAT THOU WERT THOU ART!
Gird thee with thine ancient might,
Forth, and God defend the Right!
  Henry Newbolt

There's Drake and Blake and Nelson, and 'Bobs' who pulled us through,
Now it's Kitchener and Jellicoe and George the Fifth and YOU.

The Lord help honest people and the Foul Fiend take his own,
For you shall smash the Mad Dog's head and stamp his rabbles down
And keep the old flag flying from Wick to Malabar - Oh, it's war, war, war!
By Dad's best hat, it's war.

    T.W.H. Crosland (1868-1924), journalist and writer with a considerable output of prose and verse.

Lad with the merry smile and the eyes
 Quick as a hawk's and clear as the day,
You who have counted the game, the prize,
 Here is the game of games to play.
Never a goal the Captains say -
 Matches the one that is needed now;
Put the old blazer and cap away.
 England's colours await you now.
  R.E. Vernede

When are you coming to help us,
 You that are staying at home,
Playing at golf or at cricket, leaving the fighting alone?
  Edith A. Fieldhouse

What will you lack, sonny, what will you lack,
 When the girls line up in the street,
Shouting their love to the lads come back
 From the foe they rushed to beat?
Will you send a strangled cheer to the sky
 And grin till your cheeks are red?
But what will you lack when your mate goes by
 With a girl who cuts you dead?

    Written by Harold Begbie (1871-1929), author and journalist, published in the *Daily Chronicle*, set to music by Sir Frederic Cowen (1852-1935), sold at 1*s* (5p) for the benefit of the Prince of Wales's Distress Fund.

The PRC's work was not greeted with universal approval. *The Times History of the War* speaks in one volume of 'the advertising campaign, as gigantic as it was humiliating', and in another exclaims 'very surprising and shocking ... was the discovery that the idea of serving the country had to be conveyed ... by methods of this kind.' An earthier critic, probably a recruiting officer, writing after the Military Service Acts had made recruiting posters redundant, thought them ill-conceived to appeal to 'human nature as it exists in ... the Lower Orders, and which, though not unfeeling or unpatriotic, is sub-cynical, undemonstrative, and irresponsive to cheap rhetoric and appeals to the emotions, except, perhaps, from behind the footlights.' He thought much more might be acheived by 'a poster setting forth the ... liberal scale of rations supplied to the men at the front.'.[47]

As with most advertising, there is no way of assessing the effectiveness of the torrent of printed material which flowed over war-time Britain in 1914-5. Since the recruiting figures, after the first burst of enthusiasm, were tending downwards all the time, with successive peaks always lower and successive troughs always deeper than the peaks and troughs which had gone before, it seems that a great deal of the effort was wasted, as a great deal of advertising effort always is. On the other hand it was generally felt that Kitchener's pointing finger hit hard and the poster that carried it was reproduced many times in varying forms, even to the extent of being modified for America in 1917 and revived with Churchill's head instead of Kitchener's, and the words 'Deserve Victory!' in the Second World War.[48] Of the posters in general the most that can be said is that they kept their central message - 'Join up!' - inescapably before the public eye. That is as much as can be expected of a poster and, in commercial advertising, is of considerable value.

In condemning 'cheap rhetoric and appeals to the emotions' the recruiting officer's judgment was probably sound, especially since the rhetoric and appeals included blackmail. In his reference to 'the footlights' he was no doubt thinking of recruiting concerts. They were often glamourised by leading performers. Harry Lauder (1870-1950), the Scottish ex-miner who, as a comedian, is probably best known for the song 'Glasgow belongs to me', was knighted for his efforts in 1919. Vesta Tilley (1864-1952), a tiny male impersonator who made a speciality of soldiers, was said to have caused a boom in recruiting, before the war, with the song 'Jolly Good Luck to the Girl who loves a Soldier'. Another hit was 'The Army of To-day's all right' and she was very active during the war itself.[49]

In the atmosphere of a recruiting concert 'cheap rhetoric' would go a long way, especially helped along, as it sometimes was, with rumbustious sex-appeal. At a concert to be held at 7 30 pm on 20th June 1915, in the Royal Victoria Hall opposite Waterloo Station, it was announced that after a recitation from Henry V, a 'patriotic address' by Martin Harvey (Sir John Martin-Harvey (1863-1944), actor-manager), more recitation (from Conan Doyle) and a Russian rendering by a Russian soprano of the Russian national anthem, 'Miss Edith Bracewell, after reciting "What Abaht It?" will don a recruiting sergeant's cap and walk about among the audience, picking out likely recruits.'[50]

One practitioner of 'cheap rhetoric', persistently and to large audiences, was Horatio Bottomley, who ended his career as a journalist, financier and demagogue by going to gaol for fraud in 1922.[51] In the Albert Hall on 14th January 1915, with the Vicar of Brixton in the chair, he addressed 20,000 people, 40,000 having, he said, been turned away. He hinted at dreadful scandals in the Government which he would reveal, he said, after the war. He praised the British Empire, damned the German Empire, regretted he was over military age, said many unkind things about young men who didn't enlist, and attacked a Labour MP - 'Ladies and Gentlemen, I don't want to mention the cur's name (Laughter, cheers, and cries of "traitor", "shame", and "Keir Hardie").' Having roused his audience he made a few more remarks, including an unlikely story about sailors in a sinking British ship standing in line 'saluting the old flag and singing "Tipperary" as they went down', and passed to his peroration:

> Ladies and gentlemen, it is a mighty struggle. It is a Marathon of the gods of battle, and I confess that if I were a young man of fighting age [he was fifty-five] I should yearn to be in it. I feel that those of us who cannot join the Army are at a terrible disadvantage, because I cannot think of any prouder boast for any Britisher to make when the war is over - that he took an active and vital part in ridding England and the world of a great, a hideous menace, which but for his intervention might have wiped out ... everything worth living for or dying for on the earth (loud cheers). Ladies and gentlemen, I ask those young men if they do not really feel there is a call to them.[52]

IV

In 1914-5 it must have been difficult to go far in Great Britain without coming across some sort of recruiting meeting, whether it was addressed by Asquith at Guildhall, by Bottomley in the Albert Hall, by some obscure orator on a street-corner or in a village. 'I have the Union Jack and a bell', wrote one enthusiast. 'I ring the bell and wave the Jack. A crowd is immediately gathered.'[53] Basil Williams's total of 12,000 meetings organised by the PRC works out at somewhere near twenty-five a day during the PRC's life, and the PRC was not the only body who organised them. The Imperial Maritime League, according to Lord Willoughby de Broke, its Chairman, held 1,000 meetings in country villages during the first six months of 1915. 'Lectures with lantern slides were given by thoroughly reliable operators', he said, and went on to claim that very few meetings failed to produce one to a dozen recruits in small villages. 300 men, he said, joined the Border Regiment in ten days in Westmorland, 281 joined The Buffs in Kent between 20th and 30th October 1914, presumably as a result of an earlier tour. At St Neot in Cornwall 'nearly every available man in the village, 30 in number, joined the colours.'[54]

Advice on recruiting techniques was plentifully offered. A. J. Dawson (1872-1951), an author who, unlike the majority of amateur recruiters, served in France, published *How to Help Lord Kitchener,* sponsored by *The Standard* newspaper, in 1914. *The Standard*, with War Office blessing, appealed for voluntary recruiters on 24th August 1914. They were advised to provide themselves, from a recruiting office, with details of service in Kitchener's army. 'Set to work then', Dawson went on, 'quietly, discreetly, unobtrusively, in your own locality, to induce eligible young men to offer themselves for enlistment.' Not all activities need be so subfusc. Meetings with patriotic music might be organised. 'Ladies should be specially invited to speak, and to use their influence.' The economic argument, at the working-class level, might be strong:

> It will be seen that, to take the case of a London recruit who has a wife and three children, his family, apart from his own pay and maintenance in the Army, draws something in the close neighbourhood of a pound a week. For very many working men, this means that enlistment would certainly involve no monetary loss.[55]

One method of recruiting which Dawson presented with enthusiasm came close to kidnapping. Mr Rogers-Jenkins, 'a well-known South African', went out on a Monday in his car, taking two chauffeurs and a Boy Scout. His object was to find 'unemployed men and idlers, who were picked up and driven to Fulham recruiting station.' Between Tuesday and Friday, Rogers-Jenkins said, he found 174 recruits. On Saturday 5th September 1914 *The Standard* suggested a special week-end effort, including an approach to the clergy, with the idea of getting at potential recruits in their leisure time. Each recruiter should aim at getting three men to accompany him to the recruiting office by nine o'clock on Monday morning. 'Have your three to breakfast with you,' said *The Standard* brightly. 'Make it a jolly breakfast.'[56]

Coulson Kernahan (1858-1943) was a literary man of some reputation and, as he said, 'an ex-Territorial officer', though he must have been an elderly one. He gave detailed advice in *The Experiences of a Recruiting Officer,* published in 1915 when the prospect of conscription was plain. 'Don't', he said, 'threaten those who refuse to enlist with conscription.'

At least as early as September 1914, apparently following a suggestion by an elderly retired admiral, Penrose Fitzgerald (1841-1921), women took to distributing white feathers to young men, often complete strangers, who were not in uniform.[57] Kernahan, not alone, was against white feathers: 'The woman who offers a man a white feather exposes herself, and not undeservedly, to rudeness and insult. If she do worse ... and send it anonymously by post, she thereby classes herself ... as what in the other sex would be called a "cad".' At meetings, he wanted those who conducted them to

> come down from the platform and try to get into direct personal touch with your man.... . Meetings are not infrequently held at which the speaking is powerful and convincing, and the enthusiasm great, but when a call for recruits is made, none come forward. Then some wise, tactful, well-informed man or woman may move about the crowd quietly to individual young fellows. Soon a cheer goes up as he or she walks to the recruiting officer with the first recruit ... it is always your first recruit who is hardest to secure.

Pursuing the same theme, he went on: 'Don't confine your canvassing to meetings. ... Personal canvassing brings more recruits *who could not otherwise be obtained.*' He reminded his readers that a man who refused to enlist should not be called a shirker or a coward: 'he is within his rights ... and abuse may merely make him bloody-minded.' Too much pressure might be disastrous: 'Don't forget there comes a time when ... it is well to leave your man alone. He wants to think it over, perhaps to talk it over, and in any case he may wish to feel that he has enlisted of his own choice rather than under pressure or persuasion.'[58]

'Pressure or persuasion' was everywhere, taking many forms and coming from many directions. Landowners, for instance, sought to bring pressure to bear on tenantry, their own and each other's. In January 1915 Lord Breadalbane wrote to his neighbour, Lord Bute: ' I wonder whether your Bute [Territorial] Association would very much object to us in Argyllshire getting up a recruiting party to Bute. ... We are getting up a recruiting party to send round in the hope of bucking up all the young men. I have got a very popular clergyman to form one of the party.' Even with the blessing of the Kirk, Bute regarded this proposal as poaching. He replied: 'the Bute Territorial Association meeting was held yesterday, and I fear was not in favour of men being recruited in Rothesay for Argyle.' 'But your recruiting party will not miss much,' he added maliciously, 'as there are not many men left in Rothesay, and any there may be, I expect we will want for our own Territorials.'[59] 'When the war is over', said another magnate, Lord Derby, 'I intend, as far as I possibly can, to employ nobody except men who have taken their duty at the front. I go further than that, and say that, all things being equal, if two men come to me for a farm and one has been at the front there is no doubt who is going to get the farm.'[60]

In the City of London, on 3rd September 1914, the staff of a firm of stockbrokers found themselves confronted with a written notice: 'The firm expects that all the unmarried staff under 35 years of age will join Earl Kitchener's army at once, and also urges those who are married and eligible to take the same course.'[61] This was in spite of the fact that the families who owned the firm had strong Quaker connections and might have been expected to disapprove of military service. A couple of days later, in South Wales, the general manager of the Cardiff Railway Company circulated an 'Urgent Appeal to Staff of All Grades', accompanied by a form, expressing willingness to enlist, to be filled in and returned to him. The manoeuvre succeeded embarrassingly well. By 9th September the General Manager had gone into reverse and was warning any employee who enlisted without permission that he would 'be treated as having left the Company's service and no special steps will be taken to keep his position open for him on his return from the War.'[62]

By 25th October 1915 compulsory service was plainly in view, but pressure to volunteer was still being applied. A letter sent out on that date to employees of the Post Office by the Postmaster-General had the ominous beginning: 'Dear Sir, Your name has been given to me as that of a man of military age who can be spared by the Department for Service in the Army.'[63]

Early in 1915, with the backing of the Lord Mayor of London, money was raised to form recruiting bands to accompany troops on route marches and to give 'free patriotic smoking concerts.' Waldorf Astor (1879-1952), later 2nd Viscount Astor, contributed £5,000 at once. Rudyard Kipling gave 'the entire proceeds of the sumptuously illustrated volume containing his "Song of the English" and his Mansion House Speech', besides remarking: 'a few drums and fifes in a battalion ... swing [it] back to quarters composed and happy in its mind - no matter how wet and tired its body may be.'[64] The Lord Mayor, in his 1915 Show, paraded seven batteries of artillery, a Yeomanry regiment and twenty-one battalions of infantry, besides smaller contingents of troops and nine bands.[65]

Edgar Wallace (p. 31 above) was commissioned by George Newnes to produce 'Kitchener's Army and the Territorial Force, The Full Story of a Great Achievement', published with many illustrations under the title *In the King's Army,* the cover decorated with a charging trooper. 'Ian Hay' - John Hay Beith (1876-1952) - an enthusiastic schoolmaster at a Scottish public school (Fettes), a highly, if unevenly, successful author and playwright, and an infantry officer who won the Military Cross, had enormous success with *The First Hundred Thousand,* written on service in a breezily jocular style which, repeated in 1943, did not go down so well in the very different atmosphere of the Second World War. These are only two of the authors, prominent and less prominent, who turned their abilities to the production of recruiting propaganda.

A young man might escape pressure from employers or the gentry. He

E

might read neither newspapers nor books. He might keep his eyes averted from posters and there was no compulsion to attend meetings or concerts. Even so, there would be the closest influence of all - from his family and friends. That might be decisive.

There are signs in Kernahan's book and elsewhere, including *Punch,* that emanation of the middle-class mind, of uneasiness among middle-class recruiters in approaching men of the working class. It is hardly surprising in view of the sour state of labour relations before the war in several of the country's most important industries. Disputes kept on breaking out during the war, conducted chiefly not by the official union leadership, which supported the war effort, but by shop stewards, including revolutionary socialists opposed to capitalism and all its works among which, in their view, the war took a prominent place.

Probably not many who followed revolutionary leadership were revolutionaries themselves. Indeed, in the areas of greatest militancy - South Wales and the 'red Clyde' - there were more recruits in proportion to the population than elsewhere,[66] and serious difficulties arose in shipbuilding and engineering because so many skilled men went away to the war. Those who remained then found themselves in a position of unprecedented power and it went against their whole tradition not to exploit it, especially when they knew their employers were making very large profits. Then women were brought into factories. They represented a threat both to cherished trade practices built up over many years of dour struggle and to the deep-rooted convention of male dominance, giving further cause for unrest. Men of the working class were not unpatriotic but they kept their patriotism in one part of their minds and the traditions of their working-class lives in another, in a manner difficult for the middle class to understand.

For the potential middle-class recruit the greatest obstacle to doing his patriotic duty might well be the prospect of joining Kitchener's army, explicitly an extension of the regular army, as a private soldier.

> 'Volunteering and the Territorial movement', says Edgar Wallace, 'he understood ... but the Regular Army was apart and aloof from the understanding and from all participation by the thousands of young men occupying regular positions in commercial life or entitled to describe themselves as 'independent'. Certainly these latter never thought of the Army save as an institution to be viewed through the windows of an officers' mess-room.'[67]

The Times agreed. 'It was not fear of German bullets so much as terror of British barracks', said a contributor to the Recruiting Supplement of November 1915, 'that prevented many youths from joining the Army at the beginning of the war.' One of the merits of the PRC's system of recruiting, it was held, was that 'young men of the middle class prefer to be approached ... by tactful civilians rather than by robust old soldiers of limited vocabulary.'[68]

One young man in Ireland, aged about seventeen at the outbreak of war, decided quite reasonably that his education would be wasted if he joined the army as a private. He waited a couple of years until he could go to the Royal Military Academy, Woolwich, to train for a regular commission, disregarding a pointed enquiry from a female relation, when he was eighteen, as to why he was not yet in the army.[69] Another young man, killed in 1916, indicated that a gentleman presenting himself at a recruiting station 'felt as self-conscious as if he had arrived at a dinner-party in a Norfolk jacket.'[70]

Many young men from well-to-do families must have been considerably shaken by encountering 'the lower classes' at close quarters and as equals. 'I had never met anyone before like the men in my Company', wrote P. G. Heath, a public-school boy who enlisted as a private and was later commissioned and awarded the Military Cross. 'Apart from three or four ex-public schoolboys they were a fairly rough crowd, Thames bargees, workmen and factory hands from the Clapham district. Their language was lurid, and most of them were extremely light-fingered.'[71]

Heath and many others quickly became officers. The shortage of junior officers was so great and so many were so quickly killed that a public schoolboy or anyone else of good education was unlikely to remain long in the ranks unless by his own choice. The routes to a commission were many and various. Heath got his, in November 1914, through the good offices of an elderly cousin who was a major-general at the War Office. A little later Harold Macmillan, already commissioned in the King's Royal Rifle Corps, was enabled to move to the Grenadier Guards by the help of his mother and 'the recommendation of one or two ... Oxford friends.' By 1916 a rather less haphazard system of selection and training had been established,[72] but as late as 1918 a corporal in the Royal Engineers could be transformed into a subaltern in the Royal Artillery as the result of a recommendation by his brother-in-law, already an artillery major (though by profession a solicitor), which opened the way to an officer training unit.[73] 'Of course,' Macmillan wrote of his own experience, 'readers will exclaim that it was all wrong. It was all done by influence. ... But, after all, was it so very reprehensible? The only privilege I, and many others like me, sought was that of getting ourselves killed or wounded as soon as possible.'[74]

It was taken for granted that officers should be of higher social standing than their men. 'The British soldier', wrote Edgar Wallace, who had been one, 'is more exigent even than his Prussian foeman in his demand for the well-born.'[75] Accordingly the public schools battalions and other units of similar social composition were heavily drawn upon, early in the war, for potential officers. 118 Infantry Brigade (p. 110 above) consisted entirely of public schools battalions (5,000 men in all) and while it was still in training so many men were taken from it to become officers that by the beginning of 1915 it needed 500 recruits to bring it up to strength again. 'In the case of a man wishing to serve ... with friends', said a report in the *Pall Mall Gazette* on 20th January 1915, '... every facility will be granted. ... The brigade will shortly take up its quarters in huts on Epsom Downs. No expense has been spared to make this the most up-to-date training camp in the country.'

A battalion of Artists' Rifles (28th London) was one of the earliest Territorial units to go to France. It was officially designated an 'officer-producing unit' and became, in effect, a training unit with access to the firing line. Later other units composed of 'professional men and old public school boys', such as the Civil Service Rifles and the Inns of Court Officers Training Corps, were similarly distinguished, to provide short courses of training for men recommended for commissions by their commanding officers.[76] The system was improvised, as so much that went into the making of Kitchener's armies was, it did not cover all cases, and it did not long outlast the period of voluntary enlistment. It guaranteed at least that candidates for commissions who passed through officer-producing units were nominated by sponsors who knew them as soldiers and, very often, as soldiers in battle.

During 1915 a demand grew for compulsory military service. Purely to raise troops it was probably unnecessary. 'The army', says A. J. P. Taylor, 'had more men than it could equip, and voluntary recruitment would more than fill the gap, at any rate until the end of 1916.'[77] This might have been the rational approach, but in 1915 the introduction of compulsory military service was an issue charged with emotion, as Taylor himself recognises. What people saw, or thought they saw, was not so much that men were not coming forward as that *some* men, especially men who were young and single, were not coming forward. Hence talk of 'shirkers' and 'slackers' and the distribution of white feathers. When, however, it was suggested that 'shirkers' and 'slackers' should be compelled to serve, other people grew angry also, because without much historical justification they regarded compulsory military service as an invasion of traditonal liberties.

Leaders of working-class opinion were deeply suspicious. 'We emphatically protest', runs part of a Trades Union Congress resolution of September 1915, 'against the sinister efforts of a section of the reactionary Press in formulating newspaper policies for party purposes and attempting to foist on this country conscription, which always proves a burden to the workers, and will divide the nation at a time when absolute unanimity is essential.' What the resolution meant is explained in the fifth volume of *The Times History of the War,* published not long after compulsory service passed into law: 'There was a feeling that conscription ... would be the rich man's dodge to make the poor man's son serve, and that conscription for the Army would be followed by conscription for labour purposes, forced work, low wages, and industrial servitude.'

In July 1915 the National Registration Act was passed. It required every man and woman in Great Britain, between the ages of fifteen and sixty-five, to declare, on 15th August 1915, his or her occupation. On the basis of the register thus compiled it was possible to designate 'reserved occupations' and bar men employed in them from joining the army. On the other hand those whose occupations were not 'reserved' could be identified and if compulsion were introduced they could be called up without difficulty.

On 5th October 1915 Lord Derby, who believed that compulsion would be necessary, was persuaded by Asquith and Kitchener to become Director of Recruiting and to preside over a final effort to attract volunteers.[78] Under the 'Derby Scheme' men between eighteen and forty-one were invited to 'attest' their willingness to serve when called upon. Those who attested were placed in forty-six groups according to age and marital status, the single men in groups 1 to 23 and the married in groups 24 to 46. An undertaking was given by the Prime Minister that they would be called up in that order, and particularly that married men would not be called up until after those who were single.

The Derby Scheme ran from 11th October to 11th December 1915. Men who 'attested' would avoid the disgrace of being forced into the army as conscripts and they could volunteer for immediate service if they wished. Recruiting figures rose quite sharply in October and November 1915, being helped, perhaps, by the shooting of Edith Cavell by the Germans on 12th October. Miss Cavell (1865-1915), an English nurse working in Brussels, was shot for helping French and British soldiers, cut off in Belgium, to escape into Holland, and her execution caused great public indignation. Altogether, before the end of 1915, about $2\frac{1}{4}$ million men attested and about 275,000 enlisted. After elaborate calculations, Lord Derby convinced himself that there were about a million single men who had not come forward: a figure amply large enough to justify the Military Service Act which became law in January 1916. The machinery of compulsion - the National Register and the 'Derby Groups' - was ready. All the Act had to do was to provide that from 2nd March 1916 onward all single men of military age (the married men did not escape for long) would be 'deemed to have enlisted': a neat device which made it legal to arrest any man who tried to evade his call-up.[78]

The conscription argument was fundamentally about two irreconcilable political principles: liberty and equality. So long as some men exercised their liberty not to enlist, there could be no equality of sacrifice. Here there was immense scope for invidious moral comparisons between volunteers and conscripts, and they were plentifully made. 'The choice for each of you', says a leaflet *To the Young Men of Ayrshire,* dated 12th July 1915, 'is whether you will join as a willing volunteer or wait until you are compelled. A free man enlisting will carry with him all his days the honourable pride of having done so. The conscript will get no credit either from his own conscience or from public opinion for his forced services.' In *Waiting to be Pressed,* another leaflet, a recruiting organizer says:

> It is a most singular thing that a number of likely recruits ... tell me that they are waiting to be pressed ... They do not seem to realise what their fighting ancestors did for them by building up this great and glorious Empire, and thereby recognise the duty of keeping the Empire intact ... for future generations. Surely any able-bodied man ought to consider it a privilege and honour to have the opportunity of fighting and perhaps dying for his Country in this hour of need. ....I appeal to those men to whom these words are addressed to pray to God to make them braver and better men and enable them to UPHOLD THE GLORIOUS TRADITIONS OF THE BRITISH RACE.

A leaflet under the letters OHMS ('On His Majesty's Service'), addressed to 'Men of Military Age who have not yet joined the Colours both Married and Single', says: 'If Compulsory Military Service is introduced you and you alone are responsible for forcing it upon the Country.'[79]

By the time war was imminent in 1939, public opinion on compulsory military service had altered very greatly. It was generally recognised as being the only fair method, as well as the most rational and orderly method, of raising a large army in an orderly manner instead of a chaotic rush, with the added advantage that those who were of more use at home than in the field could be kept there. Volunteers were accepted, but those who waited until they were sent for were not made to feel ashamed of themselves.

Nothing, perhaps, illustrates more vividly the difference between the spirit in which the nation went into the two great wars of the 20th century than the change in the attitude to military service. The 1914 spirit was romantic, ignorant of the horrors to come: the 1939 spirit, realistic and grim. There had been another change, too. In 1914 the nation was more concerned with liberty than with equality; in 1939 it was the other way round.

CHAPTER SEVEN

The old lie ... ?

IT'S A LONG, LONG WAY TO TIPPERARY (2).

"It's a long way to Tipperary, it's a long way to go;
It's a long way to Tipperary, to the sweetest girl
    I know;
Good-bye Piccadilly, farewell Leicester Square,
It's a long, long way to Tipperary, but my heart's
    right there."

BAMFORTH Copyright

THIS SONG ON SALE EVERYWHERE IN B. FELDMAN'S 6D. EDITIONS.

In the air of 1914 there was an ardent romanticism which had long been building up, distilled from many elements in Victorian life and culture. It carried with it an invincible belief in the superiority of all things British; hostility, tinged with fear, towards Germany seen as the great rival, upstart, efficient and unscrupulous; and an innocent vision of war as a great and gallant knightly adventure. This was a highly explosive mixture. With a slightly different balance of ingredients, without the shots at Sarajevo, the romanticism of the day might have blown the United Kingdom apart, as indeed in the summer of 1914 it seemed set to do, probably by way of civil war beginning in Ireland, possibly by some convulsion in Great Britain itself. Then Germany invaded Belgium. The force of the consequent explosion was discharged on the battlefields of France and Flanders.

This romanticism, full of the influence of nineteenth-century notions of chivalry, was strong in the ruling class, that recent Victorian amalgamation of upper-class and upper-middle-class families which held the seats of power in the nation and commanded the respect, even if sometimes grudging, of the rest of the community. Views and opinions held in the upper classes carried great weight. In the rest of the nation different views might be held and expressed, especially among the industrial working classes, but they were noises off. Working-class opinion before 1914 did not hold the centre of the stage, nor would it for half a century or more.

The social mixture which produced the rulers of Victorian England can be illustrated from the family connections of some of the wide group of friends, highly placed in London Society, which for some reason which is now totally obscure became known during the late 1880's as The Souls.[1] In the ancestry and marriages of the members of this group and their children trade, manufacturing, the professions, the landed gentry and the aristocracy were all mingled. A. J. Balfour's paternal grandfather, for instance, was a Scottish nabob and his uncle was the 3rd Marquess of Salisbury. Margot Tennant was the daughter of one of the wealthiest business men in Glasgow in Glasgow's wealthiest days. She married H. H. Asquith, a barrister who became Prime Minister and an Earl. Raymond, Asquith's son by his first wife, married a daughter of Sir John Horner whose family since the sixteenth century had owned an estate centred on Mells in Somerset. Sir John's wife Frances was the daughter of William Graham, 'a self-made merchant in the India trade'.[2] Lady Diana Manners, of the family of the Dukes of Rutland, married Alfred Duff Cooper - his father was a surgeon and his mother a duke's daughter.

Similar connections could readily be demonstrated among other groups of families highly placed in the social order. The Churchills, for example, were part of a wide-ranging network of great families including, to select a few more or less at random, Spencer, Villiers, Stanley, Ormonde, Gordon-Lennox (Dukes of Richmond).[3] In 1955 Lord Annan traced the ramifications of the 'intellectual aristocracy', in which Macaulays, Darwins, Huxleys, Trevelyans, Arnolds and many other families were inter-related.[4] This group was particularly important for its influence in scientific and university circles (by no means concentric) and, through Thomas Arnold, in the public schools. It is not going very much too far, indeed, to say that nearly all the families of wealth and influence in Victorian England were inter-related, making a very tough, closely-woven fabric at the head of society, uniting the ancient 'landed interest' with business, the professions, the public service, and education as represented by the universities and the public schools.

How numerous lines of influence could be connected in one individual by ties of birth and marriage may be illustrated by the example - many more examples could be cited - of Edward Lyttelton (1855-1942), headmaster of Eton from 1905-16 and a celebrated cricketer. He was himself an Etonian. He was the son of a peer (the fourth Baron Lyttelton). One of his brothers became a general, another a bishop, and he was connected with the Souls' circle through another brother, Alfred (colonial secretary in Balfour's Government, 1903-5), who married Laura Tennant.[5] She died almost thirty years before her husband.

The main seat of power and influence, both political and social, was in England, and particularly London. The group at the head of affairs, however, had strong connections with Scotland and with Ireland, where the protestant gentry of English and Scottish extraction, permanently insecure amid the hostility of the catholic Irish, had a strong tradition of military service - many regular officers were Irish, including two heroes of Victorian England, the Duke of Wellington and Lord Wolseley - and cherished a particularly fanatical and romantic loyalty to the Crown. It was loyalty, however, which stopped well short of any suggestion of Irish Home Rule. In 1914 opposition, concentrated in Ulster, to the Liberal Government's home rule bill, seemed to be bringing civil war very close indeed. But for the outbreak of war with Germany many officers of the British army, if the omen of the 'Curragh incident' in March 1914 is to be taken seriously, as it was at the time, might have been refusing to support the British government or even fighting against it. Fifty-seven cavalry officers, and some from the infantry, indicated that they would rather be dismissed the army than serve in Ulster in support of the Home Rule Bill.[6]

Most boys of the governing class, by 1914, went to public schools and in many cases their fathers had been to one also, often the same one, unless rising prosperity allowed them to afford somewhere better. Above Eton you could not go, and Eton had strong ties with many influential families. One of the functions of the public schools, taken very seriously, was to act informally as junior military academies. Any boy who went to one, as was suggested in Chapter Five, was likely to come under the influence of an atmosphere favourable to military service.

When war broke out, therefore, the idea of joining the army came quite naturally to men of this class: more naturally, probably, than to men lower in the social scale. This is an impression gained from the plentiful memoirs of the period which have been published.[7] Such men naturally thought of themselves as potential officers, since their education and upbringing had been designed to fit them for positions of authority and men of their class, in any case, always became officers if they took up a military career. 'The great public schools of England', wrote Edgar Wallace, 'contributed almost to their last man to the call for officers.'[8] He quotes no figures - probably he had none - but there is good reason to think he was right. From Winchester 539 boys left in the six years before 1915, and in 1915 531 had gone to the war.[9] Figures quoted by Edgar Wallace for Oxford and Cambridge, where the proportion of public schoolboys among the undergraduates was high, are large. He says that by February 1915 about 7,000 men from each university were in the army, and it appears from another source that during the whole war 13,877 men from Cambridge served and 14,171 from Oxford.[10]

From among these men, cultivated, highly articulate, steeped in classical learning as many of them were, came some of the best-known of the early war poets: Rupert Brooke (Rugby and Cambridge), C. H. Sorley (Marlborough and Oxford) Julian Grenfell (Eton and Oxford). Their verse, melodious and full of the naive enthusiasm of the day, had a great vogue. 'The fighting man shall from the sun Take warmth, and life from the glowing earth ...' wrote Julian Grenfell.[11] He was a regular cavalry officer of great bravery and having a strong taste for physical violence. The most famous poem of this *genre* - Brooke's sonnet 'The Soldier' - was published in *The Times* on 5th April 1915 and has been reprinted uncountably.

The work of later poets - Sassoon, Blunden, Owen, Gurney, Rosenberg and others - including some very noble poetry - is often taken to represent wholesale disillusionment with 'the old lie' (Owen's phrase) of pre-war patriotism, but that view must not be carried too far. It is possible to find poetry of angry disillusionment written very early in the war: poetry of pre-war idealism written not long before the armistice. Grenfell's poem, quoted above, was written 'in the firing line' and there seems every reason to suppose that Grenfell was one of those who enjoyed war even after he saw its wickedest face.[12] 'Charles Edmunds' (C. E. Carrington MC) in *A Subaltern's War* and Brigadier-General F. C. Crozier in *The Men I Killed,* a work of cold ferocity, are others who make it plain that they were very far from being broken down by the horror of it all.[13]

The early volunteers from the social level of the Souls were brought up to a way of life that has passed away. It was founded on the self-confidence of an assured position at or near the head of society; on wealth - even the poorest Souls were very rich indeed by comparison with the masses below them; on leisure (to be distinguished sharply from idleness); on everything, in fact, which is summed up in the phrase 'a gentleman of independent means'.

They had acquired the habit which railway branch-lines and later the motor-car made increasingly possible: the country-house week-end. Two of the houses which the Souls and their children frequented - Clouds in Hampshire and Taplow Court in Buckinghamshire - were modern mansions of considerable *grandeur.* Two were less pretentious but of a peculiarly English beauty, calm but almost painfully intense: the sixteenth-century, stone-built houses at Stanway in Gloucestershire and Mells in Somerset.

The church and churchyard at Mells have become a collective shrine not only to the Horners but to the Souls, their children and their circle. It is one more illustration of the wide-ranging personal links in society at this level. Laura Lyttelton, the greatest friend of Lady Horner at the manor house, is commemorated on a tablet by a favourite Souls' artist, Sir Edward Burne-Jones, devoid of christian symbolism but flourishing a very splendid peacock. Edward Horner, Sir John and Lady Horner's son, rides a bronze horse by Sir Alfred Munnings above an epitaph of eighteenth-century elegance. Although composed, probably, after the war, it expresses much of the romantic idealism of the early volunteers - and also, by implication, a county family's sense of its own position in society:

Edward William Horner
Lieutenant in the Eighteenth Hussars
Who was born on the 3rd of May 1888 and died the 21st November 1917.
He was greatly loved in his home at Mells but with eager valour he left his heritage at the outbreak of war to fight in France. Severely wounded at Ypres he recovered and returned to his regiment and fell at last in Picardy whilst defending the village of Noyelles against the German Army in the battle of Cambrai. Thus in the morning of his youth he hastened to rejoin his

friends and comrades by a swift and noble death.

A Latin inscription carved by Eric Gill into the wall of the tower records the military and academic prowess of Edward's brother-in-law Raymond Asquith, a fellow of All Souls, who was killed in 1916. In the churchyard are Siegfried Sassoon, Ronald Knox, Raymond Asquith's sister Lady Violet Bonham-Carter, and other friends, relations and servants.

Upper-class intellectual culture was founded on the tradition of 'liberal education' - that is, education for the life of a gentleman - at the greater public schools and at Oxford and Cambridge. Among the Souls and their children links with Eton and Balliol College, Oxford, were especially strong. As Raymond Asquith's epitaph was intended to indicate, it was principally an education in classical literature, history and philosophy which for those who could take full advantage of it - not the majority - provided superb mental training. If the accomplished classical scholar could also be a good games player, as some were, he would have had a very complete education, and he might expect to make a flying start into a career, probably in the public service, law or politics but probably not in anything nearer commerce or industry than banking.

The early volunteers from the upper levels of society thus moved in close-knit circles with common traditions of up-bringing and education, well aware of what was 'done' and 'not done' and with very strict and well-defined standards of behaviour. Being by no means averse to mutual admiration, and being highly articulate, they and their acquaintances wrote about each other and to each other with fluent grace, conveying to posterity the impression, which has found its place among the legends of the Great War, of a doomed 'lost generation', chiefly among the upper classes, of unparallelled physical and intellectual splendour.

Professor Gilbert Murray, after the war, wrote of 'a wonderful band of scholars' from New College Oxford. Julian Grenfell - 'one of the most complete Englishmen ever to come from Oxford' - quoted Euripides as he lay dying from a wound in the head.[14] 'Shining figures in a golden age of young men', Lord Chandos (Oliver Lyttelton) wrote of half-a-dozen old Etonians. '... I still remember the effortless scholarship and brilliance of this galaxy.'[15] Of Rupert Brooke, soon after his death, Winston Churchill wrote: 'Joyous, fearless, versatile, deeply instructed, with classic symmetry of mind and body, he was all that one would wish England's noblest sons to be.'[16]

Writers of reminiscences and obituaries are not upon their oath and we may discount the more extravagant fulsomeness. Some men of brilliance were lost: others, perhaps, of a brilliance which shines in fond memory more brightly than it shone in life. What is certain is that losses at the upper levels of society were heavy enough to foster the notion of the 'lost generation': a conclusion supported by the long 'rolls of honour' in public schools and in colleges of Oxford and Cambridge, and by the published records of individual families. In *The Children of the Souls* Jeanne MacKenzie deals with seven families, including the family of H. H. Asquith, the Prime Minister, by his first wife. In these seven families there were thirteen sons. Eight were killed. Among the wide-ranging cousinhood of the Tennants, nine were killed, including three brothers, and a tenth died in 1927 from the effects of poison gas.[17] Lord Rothermere lost two sons out of three. Two of Anthony Eden's three brothers were killed. Dr J. M. Winter's research on casualties among men from Oxford and Cambridge, a group likely to be higher than average in social standing, shows the proportion killed at 16-17 per cent (much higher in some colleges) of those who served, against 13 per cent of all men who served in the army.[18]

None of these figures, appalling though they all are, is conclusive. Losses may have been equally grievous, but less well documented, lower down the social scale, and inspection of the names on war memorials gives some support to this view. Nevertheless since the upbringing and education of men in the upper classes predisposed them to volunteer for active service, and since they mostly became junior officers, notoriously more likely to be killed than private soldiers, then there is a strong probability that losses among the upper classes were even greater, proportionately, than lower down the social scale.

Members of the ruling class of Victorian England were guilty of much that, since their time, has come to be considered reprehensible. They were proud of the British Empire. They had a lively sense of the superiority of their own class over all others in the country, and of the superiority of the British race over all others in the world. Accordingly they had no doubt of their own right to govern the lower orders and native races. In general they expected the consideration due to an *élite* of birth, wealth and culture, and they regarded with contempt most aspects of the commerce and industry by which the nation earned its living in the world.

They lived a life of privilege, took it for granted, thoroughly enjoyed it, and sometimes abused it. They did not abuse it, however, as they very easily might have done, to find safe jobs for themselves in the Great War. Their sense of privilege was balanced by an equally strong sense of duty. Bishop Welldon (p. 97 above) was right when he said that when an 'English gentleman ... is put down in the face of duty ... he will know what to do, and he will do it.' He might have extended his remarks to cover women of the same class, and never more so than during the Great War.

When Harold Macmillan (Lord Stockton)'s battalion of the Grenadier Guards left for France in August 1915, a full luncheon 'in the style of a peace-time party', presided over by the *maitre d'hotel* of the Ritz Hotel in London, was served to the officers in the troopship, having been arranged by one of the company commanders, 'a man of equal wealth and generosity.'[19] The Guards officers had their lunch, but they paid for it. They cannot be accused of failing to recognize that privilege has its price or of unwillingness to defend the things they believed in. If to later generations their patriotism has become incomprehensible - if the Great War for Civilisation has come to be considered the greatest and most barbarous of tribal wars - at least it will not be denied that the men of Kitchener's army, led by those whom most of them still considered their natural leaders, went to war not because they were compelled but because, in Cromwell's words, they 'knew what they fought for and loved what they knew.'[20]

REFERENCES

Works are cited by author's name (where applicable) and short title. For full details see Works consulted and cited.

Chapter One

1 William Collins (1721-59), 'Ode Written in the Year 1746'; Lord Erskine (1750-1823), in defence of William Stone.
2 H. O. Arnold-Foster, 'The Army and the Government', *19th Century* XLIII 346.
3 Woods (ed), *Young Winston's Wars* 47.
4 From *Punch* (n d) in Hale, *Volunteer Soldiers*
5 Escott, *England* II 259; Dunlop, *Development of the British Army* 90-1.
6 Escott, 242-3.
7 Report of the Census of 1891 38; Mitchell & Deane *Abstract* 8-10.
8 Boswell, *Life of Johnson,* 10th April 1778.
9 Mitchell & Deane as (7) 427.
10 Cunningham, *Volunteer Force* 127.
11 *Correspondence Respecting Offers.*
12 Ibid. No 18 pp 28-9.
13 Ibid. No. 4 p 3.
14 Doyle, *Great Boer War* 2.
15 Charles Duguid, 'The History of the Stock Exchange' in Hooper (ed.) *Stock Exchange* 290; Sir Wemyss Reed, *'The Newpapers', 19th Century* XLVI 860; *Cassells' Boer War* I 85.
16 *Cassells' Boer War* 329.
17 Ibid; Dunlop as (5) 101.
18 As (14) 199.
19 As (16) II 958.
20 Erskine Childers in L. S. Amery (ed) *Times History of the War in South Africa* V 250.
21 As (14) 369-70.
22 As (16) II 332-3; see also Dunlop as (5) 96-100.
23 Childers, *CIV* 104.
24 Ibid. 301.
25 RC on the War in South Africa V 114.
26 Archibald Hurd, 'Compulsory Service, the War Office Veto', *19th Century* LXIX (January 1911) 133-49.
27 *Statistics of the Military Effort* 364 379.

Chapter Two

1 To Miss Asquith, 25th February 1915, in *Collected Poems* cxxxviii; Bombardier X, *So This Was War!* 29.
2 Pound & Harmsworth, *Northcliffe* 128 137.
3 Graph, 'The London Dailies 1896-1954', published with A. P. Wadsworth, 'Newspaper Circulations 1800-1954', a paper read to the Manchester Statistical Society 9th March 1955.
4 Reader, *Professional Men* 11.
5 Graham's one-volume edition of *On War* 23 (translation modified) 47 56 121.

6   Col. F. N. Maude (ed) *On War* I v.
7   'A Song of the English' from *The Seven Seas* (1896).
8   H. F. Wyatt, 'God's Test by War', *19th Century* LXIX 591-606
9   Ibid 594.
10 Ibid 598.
11 Ibid 598-600.
12 Maud Diver, *Desmond's Daughter* Phase I ch 3 24-5.
13 Fr H. I. D. Ryder, 'The Ethics of War', *19th Century* XLV 727.
14 Newbolt, *Happy Warrior* 168.
15 *Textbook of Small Arms,* HMSO 1929 363.
16 As (13); *J Soc. Telegraph Engineers* I 38.
17 Hough, *First Sea Lord* 117-8.
18 RC on the War in South Africa 58.
19 Trythall, *'Boney' Fuller* 17-8.
20 Fuller, *The Last of the Gentlemen's Wars* 5-6.
21 John Gooch, *The Prospect of War* 38 44.
22 Sidney Lowe, 'Should Europe Disarm?', *19th Century* XLIV (October 1898) 529;
    Mahan quoted in J. M. Robertson, *Patriotism and Empire* 83.
23 Fenn, *Henty* 16 and generally.
24 Ibid 319 321; *Who was Who* I.
25 *DNB;* Warner, *The Best of British Pluck* 37; *Who was Who* V.
26 Stables, *By Sea and Land* 110.
27 Brodrick, *Memories and Impressions* 203.
28 As (23) 333-4.
29 Warner as (25) 13-4.
30 As (23) 320.
31 Doyle, *Memories and Adventures* 121 81.
32 Russell *My Diary during the last Great War* 241-6.
33 Forbes, *Barracks, Bivouacs and Battles* 307.
34 Henty, 'The Life of a Special Correspondent' in Warner as (25) 132.
35 Dawson, *Practical Journalism* 67.
36 *Who was Who* I says 1859-64 but *DNB* says he left the army in 1867.
37 W. E. Henley, memoir of G. W. Steevens prefaced to Steevens's *Things Seen* x.
38 Churchill, *Early Life* 177-9.
39 *DNB.*
40 Forbes as (33) 218-42.
41 Steevens, *With Kitchener* 273.
42 See, e g, despatch from Durban 10th March 1900 in Woods *Young Winston's Wars*
    274-87.
43 Forbes as (33) 308.
44 Ibid. 223.
45 Woods as (42) 112.
46 Steevens as (41) 264.
47 Woods as (42) 116.
48 Forbes as (33) 152.
49 Woods as (42) 279.
50 Emery, *The Red Soldier* 232 234; Steevens as (41) ch 17 pp 164 182.
51 Emery as (50) generally.
52 Wolseley, *Story of a Soldier's Life* I 69-70.
53 *DNB;* BBC Broadcast, 'The Battle of Coronel' 17th April 1975.
54 Baden-Powell, *Sport in War* 131 163.

55 Captain Edward Hutton to his father, 29th April 1879, quoted by Emery 199.
56 Hankey, *Student in Arms* 91.
57 Fuller as (20) 6.
58 Bethell (ed) *Small Wars* 85.
59 Captain Owen Wheeler, 'The British Army' in *Our Soldiers and Sailors* 10.

Chapter Three

1 *Daily Mail* 13th March 1908 3.
2 *Daily Express* 15th July 1911.
3 MacKenzie, *Propaganda and Empire* 255.
4 Reminiscences of H. D. Till; Hillcourt, *Baden-Powell* 294.
5 *Statesman's Year Book 1914* 24 250 402.
6 A. H. Adams, 'The Insularity of the English', *19th Century* LIX 674.
7 Bethell (ed) *Small Wars* 191. See also Baden-Powell, *Scouting for Boys* 1.
8 Hillcourt as (4) 259.
9 Tennyson, 'Hands all Round', *Works* 575; Report of the 1851 Census lxxxii.
10 Despatch from Nowshera 16th October 1897 in Woods (ed) *Young Winston's Wars* 65; *The Listener* 25th May 1978 659.
11 Marshall, *Empire Story* viii; Fletcher & Kipling, *A History of England* 240; *Wonder Book of Empire* 263.
12 H. F. Wyatt, 'The Ethics of Empire', *19th Century* XLI 520; Edward Dicey, 'The New American Imperialism', ibid XLIV 487.
13 Dicey as (12).
14 Doyle, *Return of the Guards* 105.
15 Bond, *Victorian Army* 66.
16 Russell, *Diary in India* 264.
17 Thompson, *London's Statues,* generally.
18 Dilke, *Greater Britain* I vii II 406 407.
19 Magnus, *Gladstone* 261-2.
20 Charles Duguid, 'The History of the Stock Exchange' in Hooper (ed) *The Stock Exchange* 211; Escott, *England* II 502; *Shorter Oxford English Dictionary* s v 'Imperialism'.
21 Seeley, *Expansion of England* 211.
22 Ibid 10.
23 Ibid 11-2 69.
24 Ibid 184.
25 Ibid 88-9.
26 Ibid 207 222 225 227 262-3 224 277.
27 Speech in London 19th January 1904; in Birmingham 12th May 1904.
28 *19th Century* XLV 725.
29 Butler *Gordon* 252.
30 Lehman, *All Sir Garnet* 292.
31 Sidney Lowe, 'The Hypocrisies of the Peace Conference', *19th Century* XLV 690-1.
32 *John Bull* 25th January 1908 74; 21st March 1908 272.
33 Woods (ed) *Young Winston's Wars* 139-40 114; Harbottle *Dictionary of Battles,* relevant entries.
34 Steevens, *With Kitchener* 166-7 325-6.
35 Alford & Sword, *The Egyptian Soudan* 234-5 291-2.
36 Henley, *Poems* 36.
37 Stone, *War Songs* iii.

38 *Peril and Patriotism* 3.
39 'Pro Rege Nostro' in Henley's *Poems* 231.
40 Kipling, *The Five Nations,* Macmillan's Pocket Kipling 214 79.
41 Steevens as (34) 166 210.
42 Thompson, *Lark Rise to Candleford* 283-4.
43 Beckett & Simpson (eds) *A Nation in Arms* 46.
44 *Horace Darwin's Shop.*
45 Dunlop, *British Army* 9.
46 Younghusband, *A Soldier's Memories* 187-8.
47 Norah Watherston, 'An Outpost of Empire', *19th Century* LXIX 150-9.

Chapter Four

1 *Our Soldiers and Sailors* 111.
2 Dilke, *British Army* 28 29.
3 Kennedy *Anglo-German Antagonism.*
4 *The Times* 9th June 1859, reprinted as 'Riflemen Form!' in Tennyson, *Works* 892.
5 Legg, *Steep Holm Guide* 29.
6 Pound & Harmsworth, *Northcliffe* 151-2 182.
7 Le Queux *The Great War in England* in 1897 16 41.
8 Ibid 116-7.
9 Ibid 326 303 327 330.
10 Kennedy as (3) 218-20.
11 Clarke, *Voices Prophesying War* 68.
12 Report of the Census of 1881 41, of 1891 65; C. C. Perry, 'Germany as an Object Lesson', *19th Century* XLV 527.
13 *19th Century* XLV 533.
14 H. Birchenough, 'The Expansion of Germany' *19th Century* XLIII 182-3.
15 *Daily Mail* 26th April 1898 4; H. M. Stanley, 'Splendid Isolation or What?' *19th Century* XLIII 878.
16 *DNB;* Seeley, *Expansion of England* 69; Halévy, *English People* Epilogue Book I 183.
17 Ensor, *England 1870-1914* 258.
18 Steinberg, *Yesterday's Deterrent* ch 4; Kennedy as (3) 223-4.
19 Hough, *First Sea Lord* 144.
20 Churchill, *World Crisis* I 172.
21 D. C. Boulger, 'British Distrust of Germany', *19th Century* LIX 7; Avebury, 'The Future of Europe', ibid LIX 422.
22 *DNB;* see also A. Boyle, *Riddle of Erskine Childers.*
23 Medlicott, *Contemporary England* 79.
24 Usborne, *Clubland Heroes,* generally.
25 Burnaby, *A Ride to Khiva;* Hillcourt, *Baden-Powell; Illustrated War News* 2nd September 1914 23; *John Bull* 26th August 1911 293.
26 Andrew, *Secret Service* 24.
27 Childers, *Riddle of the Sands* 289.
28 Hislam, *The Admiralty of the Atlantic* 141-2.
29 Quoted in Hillcourt as (25) 259 287.
30 Pound & Harmsworth, *Northcliffe* 252.
31 Andrew as (26) 34-73.
32 Morris, *The Scaremongers* 484.
33 Ensor, *England 1870-1914* 310-6 532-6; F A 'The Yellow Pirates', *Punch* 14th March 1906 188-9.

34 Robert Blatchford, *The War that was Foretold,* new and revised edn 20 August 1914, reprinted from *Daily Mail 13-23 December 1909.*

35 *John Bull* 2nd and 9th December 1911 782 818.

36 Col. the Earl of Erroll, 'Parliament and the Army', *19th Century* LIX 867. See also Major-General Sir W Knox, 'Yeoman Hopkins', ibid LXIX 569.

37 Dilke as (2) 29.

38 Hough, *First Sea Lord* 253 144; Kennedy as (3) 445-6; Palmer,*Dictionary* 251.

39 'Paper by the Secretary of State, laying down the Requirements for our Army, dated June 1, 1891', Dunlop *Development* 307.

40 Morris as (32) 38.

41 Brochure of April 1905 (3rd Edn) issued by Joseph Crosfield & Sons Ltd, Warrington, cited by permission of Unilever PLC.

42 Sidney Low, 'South African Problems and Lessons', *19th Century* XLVI 878; H. F. Wyatt, 'God's Test by War', ibid. LXIX 600.

43 H. H. Munro, *When William Came* 116.

44 'Peace' in Brooke, *Collected Poems* 5.

45 Baden-Powell, *Scouting for Boys* 264.

46 *Wonder Book of Soldiers* 173.

47 Doyle, *Great Boer War* 532; Kipling, *Traffics and Discoveries,* Macmillan's Pocket Kipling 243 269.

48 Hamley, *National Defence* 51.

49 Dunlop *Development* 54.

50 RC on Volunteer Force, Minutes of Evidence, Q1578. On the Volunteers generally, see Cunningham, *The Volunteer Force.*

51 Dunlop as (49) 57.

52 Brochure as (41).

53 Cunningham as (50) 50.

54 *Daily Mail* 2nd April 1908.

55 Major-General Sir A. B. Tulloch, 'German Trade in South America', *19th Century* LX 39-43.

56 Kipling, 'The Islanders', in *The Five Nations,* Macmillan's Pocket Kipling 133.

57 Author's recollection.

58 Cunningham as (50) 68.

59 Haldane, *Autobiography* 192-8. See also Halévy, *The Rule of Democracy* 178-80.

60 *Haldane* as (59) 192.

61 *The Times History of the War* I 130.

62 Ibid.

63 Halévy as (59) 191.

64 *Times History* as (61) VI 282.

65 Williams, *Raising and Training* 5.

Chapter Five

1 Honey, *Tom Brown's Universe* ch 4.

2 Mangan, *The Games Ethic and Imperialism.*

3 Honey as (1) 266-72.

4 Mitchell & Deane *Abstract of British Historical Statistics.*

5 Author's recollections.

6 Reader *Professional Men* 195.

7 Newsome, *Godliness and Good Learning* Introduction.

8 Eric Dunning, 'The Origins of Modern Football and the Public School Ethos', J. A. Mangan, 'Athleticism, a Case Study of the Evolution of an Educational Ideology', both in B. Simon and I. Bradley (eds), *The Victorian Public School* 170, 150-1; Mangan, *Athleticism in the Victorian and Edwardian Public School* 22-8.

9 E. M. Oakley, 'Clifton College' in *Great Public Schools* 211.

10 *Great Public Schools* 207.

11 Ibid 137 210; *Daily Express* 4th July 1911; *Times History of the War* I 132.

12 As (10) 257 126 127 213.

13 Ibid 256 328 125-6.

14 A. H. H. Maclean, *Public Schools and the War in South Africa 1809-1902*. The figures in the text are quoted or calculated from figures in Maclean's tables. The correspondence between Maclean's figure for the number of leading public schools (62) and Honey's (64), based on different criteria, is remarkable. The two lists diverge from each other as you go down the tables, and there are 14 schools listed by Honey but not by Maclean and 12 listed by Maclean but not by Honey, nearly all towards the lower end, thus again illustrating the difficulty of defining, outside a fairly small circle, exactly which schools are 'public schools'. Maclean did not study officers of the Indian Army, which put in no corporate appearance at this white men's tribal war.

15 As (10) 267 273.

16 Mangan as (8) 113 154-61.

17 L. Huxley, 'Charterhouse' in (10) 113-4

18 Farewell sermon 1879, quoted (10) 203-4.

19 Newbolt, *Happy Warrior* vii-viii.

20 Ibid vi; Stanley, *Life ... of Arnold* II 102; Girouard, *Return to Camelot* 171.

21 Girouard as (20) Preface.

22 Kipling, 'Young Men at the Manor' 'Joyous Venture' 'Old Men at Pevensey' in *Puck of Pook's Hill*.

23 Baden-Powell, *Scouting for Boys* 211 214.

24 Newbolt as (19) 174-217 (esp 176 181).

25 Ibid 275. See also Mangan as (8) 191-6.

26 Newbolt, *My World as in My Time* 63-4.

27 Honey as (1) 131.

28 Report of Public Schools Commission 253.

29 E. Scot Skirving in (10) 136.

30 *Morning Post* 22nd January 1915.

31 Bishop J. E. C. Welldon, 'The Training of an English Gentleman in the Public Schools', *19th Century* LX 407 409-10.

32 Mason, *Kipling* 35.

33 'A Little Prep' in Kipling, *Stalky & Co.*

34 As (14) 14 15.

35 Welldon as (31), also quotations following.

36 (10) 171-5.

37 Lehman, *English Poets* 28.

38 Hankey, *Student in Arms* 91.

Chapter Six

IWM - Imperial War Museum.

1 Williams, *'Raising and Training'* 6.

2 BBC Broadcast, 'The Loneliest Men'; Churchill *World Crisis* I 176.

REFERENCES

3 Reminiscences of E. C. Powell, IWM PP/MCR/37 2-3.

4 E. R. Cooper, 'Nineteen Hundred and War Time' 121 IWM MS.

5 Williams as (1) 6.

6 Churchill as (2) I 155.

7 Reader *I C I* I 214-5.

8 Dangerfield, *Strange Death* Part II ch 4, Part III ch 4.

9 Tuchman, *Proud Tower* xiv; Churchill as (2) I 176.

10 *Times History of the War* VI 284.

11 IWM K44699.

12 *Statistics of the Military Effort* 366.

13 Magnus, *Kitchener* 279 291-2; Churchill as (2) I 191-2; Haldane,*Autobiography* 279.

14 Churchill as (2) I 192.

15 Edward M. Spiers, 'The Regular Army in 1914' in Beckett & Simpson (eds) *A Nation in Arms* 57. See also Ian Beckett, 'The Territorial Force' in ibid esp 130-1.

16 As (10) VI 285.

17 Haldane as (13) 279.

18 Williams as (1) 9; as (10) VI ch 103; as (12) 364.

19 Robson *First AIF* 21 28; Mason, *Matter of Honour* 421-2.

20 Williams as (1) 8.

21 Ibid 16-9.

22 Editor *Newcastle Chronicle* to W. E. Dowding 5th March 1915, IWM K44699 9227.

23 Williams as (1) 16-19.

24 Ibid 16-18.

25 Sir William Lever to Jules Renkin 22nd December 1914, Unilever Archives LC8470.

26 *Times Recruiting Supplement* 3rd November 1915 12; Williams as (1) 16-7; Beckett & Simpson as (15) 103-5.

27 *Evening Standard* 15th January 1915.

28 *DNB; Who was Who III.*

29 Williams as (1) 18.

30 Beckett & Simpson as (15) 103.

31 As (10) VI 286.

32 Roy Douglas, 'Voluntary Enlistment in the First World War and the Work of the Parliamentary Recruiting Committee'. *J Modern History* 42 564-85.

33 Haste, *Home Fires* 53.

34 As (31).

35 Douglas as (32) 567.

36 *Who was Who* VI.

37 Douglas as (32) 575; as (26) 4.

38 Williams as (1) 14-5.

39 As (26) 4.

40 Williams as (1) 16.

41 Haste as (33) 51-2.

42 Douglas as (32) 571.

43 Darracott & Loftus, *First World War Posters;* Hardie & Sabin, *War Posters.*

44 IWM K33304.

45 *Who was Who* V.

46 IWM K33304 46108 49977 40902.

47 As (10) I 286 V 295; W T., 'From a Recruiting Officer's Note Book' *J Royal United Services Iinstitution* LXI 831.

48 Darracott & Loftus as (43) 64.

49 *DNB.*

50 *Daily Telegraph* 19th June 1915 IWM K44699 9227.

51 *DNB.*

52 IWM K41167.

53 Dawson, *How to Help Lord Kitchener* 50.

54 Lord Willoughby de Broke, circular letter 4th June 1915, IWM K44699.

55 Dawson as (53) 17 34 43.

56 Ibid 52 95.

57 *The Times* 2nd September 1914; Haste as (33) 56.

58 Kernahan (ed), *The Experiences of a Recruiting Officer* 69-73.

59 Letters between Lord Breadalbane and Lord Bute 11th 19th January 1915, IWM K44699.

60 Churchill, *Lord Derby* 184.

61 Archives of Messrs Foster & Braithwaite, stockbrokers.

62 IWM K44699.

63 IWM K39815.

64 Douglas Sladen, 'The Story of the Lord Mayor's Recruiting Bands', in (58) 98-109.

65 *Daily Graphic* 9th November 1915.

66 Taylor, *English History 1914-45* 39.

67 Wallace, *In the King's Army* 15-6.

68 As (26) 13.

69 Reminiscences of Lt-Col W. V. C. Maffett RA (retd).

70 Hankey, *Student in Arms* 27.

71 IWM DS/MISC/60.

72 Beckett & Simpson as (15) 80.

73 Reminiscences of T. R. Till.

74 Macmillan, *Winds of Change* 63-4.

75 Wallace as (67) 186.

76 *Morning Post* 16th January 1915; *Pall Mall Gazette* 31st January 1915; Wallace as (67) 175 187; Beckett & Simpson as (15) 79-80.

77 Taylor as (66) 53.

78 As (10) V; Williams as (1) 21-7; As (10) VI ch 103.

79 IWM K44699.

Chapter Seven

1 Abdy & Gere, *The Souls* 10.

2 MacKenzie, *The Children of the Souls* 18.

3 Churchill, *Winston S Churchill* I, genealogical tables at the end of the book.

4 N. G. Annan, 'The Intellectual Aristocracy' in Plumb (ed) *Studies in Social History* 243-87. *DNB.*

6 Curragh Incident' in Palmer, *Dictionary of Modern History;* see also A. T. Q. Stewart, *The Ulster Crisis* ch 13.

7 See eg: Macmillan *Winds of Change*, Eden *Another World*, Cooper, *Old Men Forget*.

8 Wallace, *In the King's Army* 186.

9 Pound, *The Lost Generation* 151.

10 Wallace as (8) 186; Carey (ed) *War List of the University of Cambridge;* Craig & Gibson (eds) *Oxford University Roll of Service*.

11 Julian Grenfell, 'Into Battle'.

12 MacKenzie as (2) 184.

13 'Charles Edmunds' *A Subaltern's War*, F. C. Crozier, *The Men I Killed*.

REFERENCES

14 MacKenzie as (2) 185.
15 Pound as (9) 148 159 107.
16 *The Times* 26th April 1915.
17 Crathorne, *Tennant's Stalk* ix.
18 Winter, *The Great War and the British People* 93.
19 Macmillan as (7) 68.
20 Letter of September 1643 in Carlyle *Letters and Speeches of Oliver Cromwell*.

Abdy, Jane, and Gere, Charlotte, *The Souls* (Sidgwick and Jackson, 1984)

Alexander, Michael, *The True Blue: The Life and Adventures of Col. Fred Burnaby 1842-85* (Rupert Hart-Davis, 1957)

Alford, Henry S.L., and Sword, W. Dennistoun, *The Egyptian Soudan: its Loss and Recovery* (Macmillan, 1898)

Andrew, Christopher, *Secret Service: The Making of the British Intelligence Community* (Heinemann, 1985)

Annuals, *1914 illustrated, the Book of the Year* (one of a series annually from 1909) (London and Manchester: Daily News and Leader, Headley Bros, n.d.)

Anon., *Life of General Gordon* (Walter Scott, London, 1885)

Anon., *The Pictorial History of the British Empire, Social Descriptive and Biographical* (London: Thomas Mitchell, PSA Book Saloon, n.d.)

Baden-Powell, Robert *The Downfall of Prempeh* (Methuen, 1896)

Baden-Powell, Robert *Scouting for Boys: A Handbook for Instruction in Good Citizenship* (C. Arthur Pearson, 34th edn 1963 [1st edn 1908])

Beckett, Ian, The Nation in Arms, 1914-1918. See Beckett and Simpson (eds), *A Nation in Arms*

Beckett, Ian, The Territorial Force. See Beckett and Simpson (eds), *A Nation in Arms*

Beckett, Ian, and Simpson, Keith (eds), *A Nation in Arms: A Social Study of the British Army in the First World War* (Manchester University Press, 1985)

Beresford, Lord Charles, and Wilson, H.W., *Ironclads in Action* (Harmsworth Bros, n.d.)

Bethell, Lieut-Col. L.A. (ed), *'Blackwood', Tales from the Outposts*, II, *Small Wars of the Empire* (Blackwood, 1932)

Bethell, Lieut-Col. L.A. (ed), *'Blackwood', Tales from the Outposts*, VII, *Soldiers' Tales* (Blackwood, 1933)

Blake, J.P. (ed), *Official Regulations for the Volunteer Training Corps* (W.H. Smith, Wymans, 1915)

Blatchford, Robert, *The War that was Foretold* (New and Revised ed August 1914) (Reprinted from *The Daily Mail* 13-23 December, 1909)

Bombardier 'X', *So this was War!* (Hutchinson, 1930)

Bond, Brian, *The Victorian Army and the Staff College 1853-1914* (Eyre Methuen, 1972)

Boyle, Andrew, *The Riddle of Erskine Childers* (Hutchinson, 1977)

Brooke, Rupert, *The Collected Poems of Rupert Brooke, with a Memoir* (Sidgwick and Jackson, 1918)

Buchan, John, *The Thirty-Nine Steps* (1915), *Greenmantle* (1916), *Mr Standfast* (1919)

Burnaby, Captain F., *A Ride to Khiva* (Cassel Petter and Galpin, 2nd edn 1876)

Butler, Sir William, *Charles George Gordon* (Macmillan, 1903) (1st edn 1889, 10th reprint)

Cassell's History of the Boer War 1899-1902 (Cassell and Co. Ltd, 2 vols, n.d.)

Cattermole, M.J., and Wolfe, A.F., *Horace Darwin's Shop: a History of Cambridge Scientific Instrument Company 1878-1968* (Adam Hilager, 1987)

Chamberlain, Joseph, *Patriotism*. An address delivered to the Students of the University of Glasgow...on November 3rd, 1897, on the occasion of his installation as Lord Rector, (Constable, 1897)

Childers, R. Erskine, *In the Ranks of the CIV* (Smith, Elder and Co, 1900)

Childers, R. Erskine, *The Riddle of the Sands: A Record of Secret Service*, 26th impression (Sidgwick and Jackson, 1949 [1st edn Smith, Elder, and Co, May 1903])

Churchill, Randolph, *Lord Derby — 'King of Lancashire'* (Heinemann, 1959)

Churchill, Lieut-Col. Seton, *General Gordon, a Christian Hero* (Nisbet, n.d.)

Churchill, W.S., *My Early Life* (Macmillan, 1931), *The World Crisis 1911-1918* new edn, 2 vols (Odhams, 1938), *Young Winston's Wars* (ed. Frederick Woods) (Leo Cooper, 1972)

Clarke, I.F., *Voices Prophesying War* (Oxford University Press, 1966)

Clarke, J. Erskine, *Going for a Soldier and Other Tales* (Wells, Gardner, Darton and Co, 1899)

Clausewitz, Carl von, *On War*, 3 vols translated by Col. J.J. Graham (Trübner, 1873), new and revised edn, 3 vols with Introduction and notes by Col. F. N. Maude (Kegan Paul, Trench, Trübner, 1908)

Collections

Peril and Patriotism: True Tales of Heroic Deeds and Startling Adventures, Introduction by H.O. Arnold-Foster, MP (Cassell, 1901)

At Duty's Call, Stories by Gordon Stables, Harold Bindloss, A.E. Johnson, C.E. Gouldsburg, Duncan McLaren, Frank Savile, S.A. Parkes, F.S. Bowley (John F. Shaw, n.d. [c.1905])

Our Soldiers and Sailors: The Empire's Defenders in War and Peace, with 22 coloured plates and 600 illustrations (Ward, Lock, n.d. [pre-1914])

The Wonder Book of Empire (Ward, Lock, n.d. [pre-1914 text probably published during the Great War])

Cooper, A. Duff, *Old Men Forget* (Rupert Hart-Davis, 1953)

Cousins, Geoffrey, *The Defenders: A History of the British Volunteer* (Frederick Muller, 1968)

Crozier, Brig-Gen. F.P., *The Men I Killed* (Michael Joseph, 1937)

Cunningham, Hugh, *The Volunteer Force* (Croom Helm, 1975)

Darracott, Joseph and Loftus, Belinda, *First World War Posters* (Imperial War Museum, 1972)

Dawson, A.J., *How to help Lord Kitchener* (Hodder and Stoughton, 1914)

Dawson, John, *Practical Journalism, how to enter thereon and succeed* (L. Upcott Gill, Strand, n.d.)

Dilke, Sir Charles, *Greater Britain — A record of Travel in English-speaking countries during 1866 and 1867* 2 vols (Macmillan, 1868)

Dilke, Sir Charles, *The British Army* (Chapman and Hall, 1888)

Diver, Maud, *Captain Desmond VC* (Edinburgh and London: Blackwood, 1908); *The Hero of Herat* (Edinburgh and London: Blackwood, 1912); *Desmond's Daughter* (Edinburgh and London: Blackwood, 1916)

Doyle, A. Conan *The Great Boer War* (Smith, Elder, 4th Impression 1900)

Dunlop, John K., *The Development of the British Army 1899-1914* (Methuen, 1938)

Eden, Anthony, *Another World 1897-1917* (Allen Lane, 1976)

Edmonds, Charles, *A Subaltern's War* (Peter Davies, 1929)

Emery, Frank, *The Red Soldier: Letters from the Zulu War, 1879* (Hodder and Stoughton, 1977)

Escott, T.H.S., *England: its People, Polity and Pursuits* 2 vols (Cassell, Petter, Galpin and Co, n.d.)

Farwell, Byron E., *The Great Boer War* (Allen Lane, 1977)

Fenn, G. Manville, *George Alfred Henty: The Story of an Active Life* (Blackie, 1907)

Fitchett, W.H., *Fights for the Flag*, 2nd impression (Smith, Elder, 1898); *Deeds that won the Empire*, 12th edn (Smith, Elder, 1900)

Fletcher, C.R.L. and Kipling, R., *A History of England*, new edn, revised and coloured (Oxford: Clarendon Press; London; Hodder and Stoughton, 1911)

Forbes, Archibald, *Barracks, Bivouacs and Battles* (Macmillan, 1892)

Forbes-Mitchell, William, *Reminiscences of the Great Mutiny 1857-59* (Macmillan, 1895)

Fuller, Major-General J.F.C., *The Last of the Gentlemen's Wars* (Faber and Faber, 1937)

Girouard, Mark, *The Return to Camelot — Chivalry and the English Gentleman* (Yale University Press, 1981)

Gooch, John, *The Prospect of War* (Cass, 1981)

Grainger, J.H., *Patriotisms: Britain 1900-1939* (Routledge and Kegan Paul, 1986)

Great Public Schools (Arnold, n.d.)

Hale, M.H., *Volunteer Soldiers* 2nd edn (Kegan Paul, Trench, Trübner, 1900)

Hamley, Sir Edward, *National Defence — Articles and Speeches* (Blackwood, 1889)

Hankey, Donald, *A Student in Arms* (Andrew Melrose, 1917)

Haste, Cate, *Keep the Home Fires Burning* (Allen Lane, 1978)

Hay, Ian, *The First Hundred Thousand* (Blackwood, 1916)

Henley, W.E. *Lyra Heroica, a Book of Verse for Boys* (Macmillan, 1921 [1st edn 1891]); *Poems* (David Nutt, London, 1898)

Hillcourt, William, *Baden-Powell, The Two Lives of a Hero* (with Olave, Lady Baden-Powell) (Heinemann, 1964)

Hislam, Percival A., *The Admiralty of the Atlantic: An Enquiry into the Development of German Sea Power Past, Present and Prospective* (Longmans, Green, 1908)

HMSO *Statistics of the Military Effort of the British Empire 1914-1920* (HMSO, 1922)

Honey, J.R. de S. *Tom Brown's Universe* (Millington, 1977)

Hough, Richard, *First Sea Lord: An Authorized Biography of Lord Fisher* (Allen and Unwin, 1969)

Howarth, Patrick, *Play Up and Play the Game* (Eyre Methuen, 1973)

Hughes, Clive, 'The New Armies'. See Beckett and Simpson (eds), *A Nation in Arms*

Inglis, The Hon. Lady, *The Siege of Lucknow* (James R. Osgood, McIlvaine and Co, 1893)

Innes, A.D., *A History of the British Nation* (T.C. and E.C. Jack, 1912)

Kennedy, Paul M., *The Rise of the Anglo-German Antagonism 1860-1914* (George Allen and Unwin, 1980-82)

Kernahan, Coulson, *The Experiences of a Recruiting Officer* (Hodder and Stoughton, 1915)

Kingston, W.H.G., *Our Sailors: Anecdotes of the Engagements and Gallant Deeds of the British Navy during the Reign of Her Majesty Queen Victoria*, new edn, Griffith Farran & Co, n.d.); *How Britannia came to Rule the Waves* (Gall and Inglis, n.d. [not before 1876])

Kipling, Rudyard, *Plain Tales from the Hills, Soldiers Three, Wee Willie Winkie, Life's Handicap, Many Inventions, The Day's Work, Stalky and Co, The Five Nations, Traffics and Discoveries, Puck of Pook's Hill, Rewards and Fairies, A Diversity of Creatures, Debits and Credits, Kim, The Seven Seas*; also *The Jungle Book, The Second Jungle Book, The Just-So Stories* (Macmillan, various dates and editions, 1888-1926)

MacKenzie, Jeanne, *The Children of the Souls* (Chatto and Windus, 1986)

MacKenzie, John M., *Propaganda and Empire* (Manchester University Press, 1984)

Maclean, A.H.H., *Public Schools and the War in South Africa* (Edward Stanford, 1903)

Magnus, Philip, *Kitchener — Portrait of an Imperialist* (John Murray, 1958)

Mangan, J.A., *Athleticism in the Victorian and Edwardian Public School* (Cambridge University Press, 1981)

Marsh, Sir Edward, *Memoir of Rupert Brooke.* See *The Collected Poems of Rupert Brooke*

Marshall, H.E., *Our Empire Story* (T.C. and E.C. Jack, n.d. [1908]); *Our Island Story* (Nelson, n.d.)

Mason, Philip, *A Matter of Honour. An account of the Indian Army, its officers and men* (Cape, 1974)

Mason, Philip, *Kipling: The Glass, the Shadow and the Fire* (Cape, 1975)

Morris, A.J.A., *The Scaremongers: The Advocacy of War and Rearmament 1896-1914* (Routledge and Kegan Paul, 1984)

Munro, H.H. ('Saki'), *When William Came* (John Lane, The Bodley Head, 1914)

Newbolt, Sir Henry, *The Old Country* (Smith, Elder, 1906); *Clifton Chapel and other School Poems* (John Murray, 1909); *Poems: New and Old* (John Murray, 1912); *The Book of the Happy Warrior* (Longman, 1917); *My World as in my Time* (Faber and Faber, 1932)

Owen, Wilfred, *The Poems of Wilfred Owen*, ed. with a memoir and notes by Edmund Blunden (Chatto and Windus, 1933)

Palmer, A.W., *A Dictionary of Modern History 1789-1945* (Cresset Press, 1962)

Parker, Peter, *The Old Lie: The Great War and the Public School Ethos* (Constable, 1987)

Parliamentary papers

Report of the Commissioners appointed to inquire into the Condition of the Volunteer Force in Great Britain (HMSO, 1862)

Report of the Public Schools Commission (BPP. 1864),xx

Correspondence respecting the Offers by the Colonies of Troops for Service in the Soudan, C4437/ 1885 (in continuation of C4324 of March 1885)

Report of H.M. Commissioners [on]...the War in South Africa, Cd 1789/1903

Periodicals

The Boy's Own Paper
The Daily Express
The Daily Mail
Illustrated War News
John Bull
Journal of Modern History 42 (March-December, 1970), pp. 564-85, Roy Douglas, 'Voluntary enlistment in the First World War and the work of the Parliamentary Recruiting Committee'.

The nineteenth century and after

Punch

The Times, The Times Recruiting Supplement 3, November 1915

Pimblett, W., *How the British Won India* (J.S. Virtue, 1895)

Plumb, J.H. (ed), *Studies in Social History* (Longman, 1955)

Pound, Reginald, *The Lost Generation* (Constable, 1964)

Price, Richard, *An Imperial War and the British Working Class* (Routledge and Kegan Paul, and University of Toronto Press, 1972)

Punch, Mr Punch's History of the Great War (Cassell, 1920)

Richards, Frank, *Old Soldier Sahib* (Faber and Faber, 1936)

'Richards, Frank', *The Autobiography of Frank Richards* (Charles Skilton, 1952)

Roberts of Kandahar, Lord, *Forty-one Years in India, from Subaltern to Commander-in-Chief*, 5th edn, 2 vols (Richard Bentley, 1897)

Robertson, J.M., *Patriotism and Empire* (Grant Richards, 1899)

Robson, L.L., *The First AIF* (Melbourne University Press, 1970)

Ryder, Rowland, *Edith Cavell* (Hamish Hamilton, 1975)

Simpson, Keith, 'The Officers'. See Beckett and Simpson (eds), *A Nation in Arms*

Smith, G. Barnett, *General Gordon: The Christian Soldier and Hero* (Partridge, n.d.)

Smith, R. Bosworth, *Life of Lord Lawrence*, 3rd edn, 2 vols (Smith, Elder, 1883)

Spiers, Edward M., 'The Regular Army in 1914'. See Beckett and Simpson (eds), *A Nation in Arms*

Stables, Gordon, MD, RN, *By Sea and Land: A Tale of the Blue and Scarlet* (Frederick Warne, n.d. [1898?])

Stanley, Arthur Penrhyn, *The Life and Correspondence of Thomas Arnold DD*, 13th edn, 2 vols (John Murray, 1882)

Steel, Flora Annie, *The Potter's Thumb* (1894); *On the Face of the Waters* (1896)

Steevens, G.W., *With Kitchener to Khartum*, 11th edn (Blackwood, 1898); *In India* (Blackwood, 1899); *Things Seen, with a Memoir by W.E. Henley* (Blackwood, 1900)

Steinberg, Jonathan, *Yesterday's Deterrent: Tirpitz and the Birth of the German Battle Fleet* (Macdonald, 1965)

Stewart, A.T.Q., *The Ulster Crisis* (Faber and Faber, 1967)

Stone, Christopher (ed.), *War Songs*, selected by Christopher Stone with an Introduction by General Sir Ian Hamilton (Clarendon, 1908)

Simon, Brian and Bradley,Ian (eds), *The Victorian Public School* (Gill and Macmillan, 1975)

The Times Diary and History of the War (The Times Publishing Co Ltd, n.d.)

The Times History of the War, I (n.d.); V (1915); VI (1916)

Trollope, Joanna, *Britannia's Daughters* (Hutchinson, 1983)

Trotter, Captain Lionel J., *Life of John Nicholson*, 6th edn (John Murray, 1898); *The Bayard of India: A Life of General Sir James Outram*, Everyman Edn (Dent, 1909, [1st edn 1903])

Tuchman, Barbara, *The Proud Tower* (Hamish Hamilton, 1966)

Usborne, Richard, *Clubland Heroes*, revised edn (Barrie and Jenkins, 1974)

Warner, Philip, *The Best of British Pluck* (Macdonald and Jane's 1976)

Weber, Eugen, *Peasants into Frenchmen: The Modernization of Rural France 1870-1914* (Chatto and Windus, 1977)

War Office, *Textbook of Small Arms* (HMSO, 1929)

Williams, Basil, *Raising and Training the New Armies* (Constable, 1918)

Wilson, H.W., and Hammerton, J.A., *The Great War*, vol 5 (Amalgamated Press, 1916)

Winter, Jay, 'Army and Society: the demographic context'. See Beckett and Simpson (eds), *A Nation in Arms*

Winter, Jay, *The Great War and the British People* (Macmillan, 1985)

Wolseley, Field-Marshal, Viscount, *The Story of a Soldier's Life,* 2 vols (Constable, 1903)

Wood, Sir Evelyn, *From Midshipman to Field-Marshal*, 5th edn (Methuen, 1907 [1st edn, October, 1906])

Woods, Frederick (ed.), *Young Winston's Wars: The Original Despatches of Winston S. Churchill, War Correspondent 1897-1900* (Leo Cooper Ltd, 1972)

Younghusband, Major General Sir George, *The Story of the Guides* (Macmillan, 1909); *A Soldier's Memories in Peace and War* (Herbert Jenkins, 1917)

INDEX

INDEX